MW00988793

Beloved Unbeliever
Loving Your Husband Into the Faith

Jo Berry

ZONDERVAN PUBLISHING HOUSE
OF THE ZONDERVAN CORPORATION
GRAND RAPIDS, MICHIGAN 49506

Unless otherwise specified, Scripture references are from
New American Standard Bible

Additional versions are:
The Amplified Bible
King James Version (KJV)
The Living Bible (LB)

Library of Congress Cataloging in Publication Data

Berry, Jo.
    Beloved unbeliever.

    1. Wives—religious life.   2. Witness bearing
(Christianity)   I. Title.
BV4527.B46   248.8/435   81-4518
ISBN 0-310-42621-9   AACR2

Designed and edited by Louise H. Rock

Printed in the United States of America

82 83 84 85 86 87 88 — 10 9 8 7

Contents

Preface

One of the most grievous and difficult situations a Christian woman ever faces is that of being unequally yoked: being married to a man who is not a believer. Whether she was knowingly disobedient to Paul's admonition in 2 Corinthians 6:14 (KJV), "Be ye not unequally yoked together with unbelievers," or converted after her marriage, she is in a hard, and sometimes heartbreaking position.

She is supposed to live according to the dictates of Scripture, to be a helpmeet and submissive wife, yet at the same time she carries the burden of knowing her husband is neither spiritually awakened nor secure for eternity. She and her husband probably differ sharply about what their lifestyle should be. Many women in this position have shared with me that they feel hopeless.

That is the main reason I am writing this book. There is hope! There are principles an unequally yoked wife can learn and apply that will make her life easier. She needs to realize that God has placed her in the unique position of being His representative to the man she loves.

She can also develop a positive mind-set about her mate and her marriage. I have found that most unequally yoked wives resent the fact that their husbands are not Christians. The wife unknowingly lets the fact of her husband's unbelief predominate their relationship, thus stifling other facets of their marriage.

Although there are no simple answers to this dilemma, there are positive ways to approach the problem of being unequally yoked. This book contains workshop material which will help the unequally yoked woman think through her own personal situation and decide how to make necessary changes. I pray it will help her appreciate and enjoy her position as a wife.

—*Jo Berry*

Acknowledgments

Thanks to the many men and women who answered questions and opened their hearts to me. Although all the incidents described in the book are true, most names have been changed to protect their identities.

Special thanks to the women who took many hours filling out in detail the long questionnaire form. You know who you are and so does the Lord. Without your help and insights this book would not have been possible.

What Is Unequally Yoked?

One of the favorite events at the Little League picnic was a father/son three-legged race. Tall, bony men had their legs tied to those of short, chubby nine-year-olds. Heavy-set dads were hitched to their wiry sons. When "Get on your mark, get set, GO!" resounded in the park, those of us who were on the sidelines watched the contest with great amusement. Many of us laughed so hard we got tears in our eyes.

Some fathers and sons fell down before they went far. Others kept pace for a while, then one or the other stumbled. There was no doubt that the kids got the worst of things. The team who won did so because the father literally dragged his son along behind him. The boy was resisting, yelling, "Stop! Com'on dad! I want to stop!"

But the father ignored his son's pleas. He just put his head down and plunged ahead. They both toppled to the ground and hugged each other, laughing, when the event was finished.

It was amusing for those fathers and sons to be linked together in that race, as mismatched as they were in size, stamina, and capability. But I noticed that the first thing each couple did, when they either dropped out or crossed the finish line, was untie the cords that were binding them together.

I wonder how many of them would have considered staying tied together for the rest of their lives? Despite the fact that the race had been fun, it was obvious that the contestants had been uncomfortable when they were harnessed to one another.

Think about what it would be like to be permanently attached to someone who is not your equal; who you either have to run and struggle to keep pace with or who forces you to pull an inordinate share of the load. Doesn't sound like much fun, does it? That is what it means to be unequally yoked.

WHAT IS UNEQUALLY YOKED?

Unequally yoked is a biblical term. It is used only once in Scripture, when the apostle Paul, in 2 Corinthians 6:14, admonishes Christians not to "be bound together with unbelievers." The literal Greek translation of the term means to be paired with another kind: coupled to someone of a different sort.

In our mobilized society we are not familiar with the yoke. In the days when Scripture was written, oxen were beasts of burden and the yoke was a commonplace fixture. It consisted of a wooden frame or bar with loops at either end and was used to hold the animals' heads in place and maintain balance between them. The yoke was fitted around the necks of a pair of oxen, harnessing them together, making a team.

It is interesting how a yoke works. It was constructed so as to force each ox to pull an equal share of the load. It bound the animals together. Consequently, if one pulled ahead or held back, the other member of the team was hindered. The yoke actually caused pain, choking the one who pulled ahead or pinching the neck of the one who lagged behind. Because of this discomfort and the restrictiveness of the yoke, the oxen usually kept a common pace, moving in the same manner and traveling in the same direction.

So, when Paul uses the term "unequally yoked," he is implying that if a Christian teams up with an unbeliever, the pairing will hinder his walk with the Lord, restrict his freedom in Christ, and cause an imbalance of responsibility in the relationship.

Women who are in this position will attest to the truth of this principle. They are united in a permanent marriage union with someone who is not spiritually their equal. So they are burdened with an overload of spiritual responsibility. They are faced with the tremendous task of having to live a holy, exemplary life beside someone who is impure in the Lord's sight and is part of the worldly system.

Sometimes they are dragged into situations in which they want no part. But they are yoked. Sometimes they are pulled against their will toward things they believe are degrading or unseemly for a Christian. But they are yoked. They have a difficult time walking the path of righteousness because the ones to whom they are harnessed are following the way of the world. But they are yoked.

Frequently they feel they must draw back, creating conflict and friction, and they are hurt or wounded. Or, they grow weary at heart from the heaviness of the burden. Should you ask them if they are relaxed in their marriages, they would tell you they are not. They may be happy but they are not comfortable because they are unequally yoked.

How could such an inequitable pairing happen to a Christian woman? Did each one who is married to an unbeliever purposely and deliberately disobey God's command? How does someone get into this predicament? There are four ways a believer can become unequally yoked.

GOD WINS THE WIFE INTO HIS FAMILY

The first way is, I believe, the most common. An unbeliever marries another unbeliever, then at some point comes to the Lord. She becomes unequally yoked as a result of her salvation. This is the case with the majority of women I have interviewed or counseled through the years.

It is vitally important to realize that there is no disobedience involved on the part of the woman whose status is established this way. She did not have a relationship with Christ when she married, therefore she cannot be held accountable in any way for not adhering to the admonition in 2 Corinthians 6:14 (KJV) to not be unequally yoked.

Rather than disobedience, we see the sovereignty of God at work in this positioning. The Lord, who is a self-determining personality, chose to woo and win the wife into His family and not to draw the unbelieving husband to Him at the same time. Obviously, the Lord exercised His perfect will when the woman was converted.

Too often those of us in the body of Christ do not distinguish this fact. We assume that all women who are unequally yoked got that way because they married out of the will of God. That is not so. A vast majority of unequally yoked wives find the Lord after they are married.

Dana was caught in this quandary. I asked her to tell me how she reacted to her marriage after she received Christ. She said that at first she did not know enough about the Bible to realize that God drew a distinction between an unequal match and two Christians who are married.

"When I found this out I was devastated. I felt guilty. In a way, I was almost sorry I was saved. I felt as if I had deserted my husband. Then I was struck with the awful truth that every unequally yoked wife has to face, whether she married in disobedience or if God ordained her to be that way, and that is that if my husband dies he will go to hell.

"That is still the worst part of it all," she continued. "I so much want Clint to know the love of God the way I do. I cannot bear the thought of him spending eternity apart from me and our children and the Lord. I am just depending on God to finish the job He started when He drew me into the fold. I know that some day Clint will become a Christian."

I pray that Dana is right. She well may be. I know of many instances like this in which husbands have come to Christ after their wives were converted. It appears that often God chooses for the wife to come first, then uses her as the instrument of her husband's salvation. One woman I know recently had the privilege of holding her husband in her arms and leading him in his prayer of confession of faith in Christ. Another was cooking dinner when her husband strolled into the kitchen and calmly announced that he wanted to become a Christian. She had been waiting for eight years to hear those words.

So, it seems that wives who marry as unbelievers, then come to the Lord, frequently are used as the tool of salvation for their spouses. But, each one I know has told me that it did not happen overnight. She had to "prove" herself and the workability of her faith to her mate by living her Christianity.

She had to learn what God expects from a godly wife and mother, then consistently practice those ideals before her husband responded. This underlines the importance of obedience and should be an encouragement to women in such circumstances.

HE'S NOT WHAT HE SEEMS

A second way a woman can become unequally yoked is to marry a non-Christian, thinking he is a believer when he is not. Although there may be a lack of discernment on her part, she honestly believes she is marrying a Christian. I know of instances where the unbeliever actually thought he had accepted Christ, where the minister who performed the ceremony was convinced the groom was saved, and where family and friends of the couple accepted him as part of the fellowship.

Sometimes an unbeliever will purposely pretend to confess Christ so the Christian woman will marry him. He deceives her. In either case, these men "play the game" well. Many give superficial evidence of conversion. They seem to bear fruit. They go to church, use the language, and read the Bible. But, they are not saved.

Jolene was caught in such a plight. She says she was totally convinced that Dan was a Christian. She even met him at a church camp. He had come with a friend. She and Dan had a big church wedding with all the trimmings. But when they settled down to the process of everyday living, he started withdrawing from the things of the faith. It got so bad that he told Jolene he didn't want her bugging him about going to church and that if she went he didn't want to hear about the sermons or Bible lessons.

When I asked her how she felt when she realized Dan was not saved, she said, "When the truth dawned on me I got physically sick. First I fooled myself into thinking Dan was just being carnal. I counseled with the pastor and a woman friend. Both of them told me I shouldn't judge his Christianity but pray for his growth. That made me feel guilty.

"But as time passed, I realized he did not have the desire for Christ that I have, and he had no conviction. His thinking patterns were so contrary to scriptural ones, and his attitude toward me changed so drastically, that I knew he wasn't saved. There was a real war of the souls between us. We were at opposite ends of the pole when it came to the things of God, so we were in opposition to each other in a lot of matters.

"Finally, one night when he came home drunk I started crying hysterically and asked him how he could have lied to me about being a believer. He told me it was because he didn't want to lose me. He thought he could handle the religion bit, but found out he couldn't. We talked all night that night and laid some ground rules so our whole marriage wouldn't go on the rocks. But I can tell you, I was so discouraged I almost died.

"I was also embarrassed in front of my Christian friends to admit I had been so stupid. One of them reminded me that everyone had been taken in by Dan's performance. I don't know if he will ever come to Christ. I am so fearful because he knew so much and then rejected it. It's not as if he didn't have any knowledge or understanding of the Scriptures. He knows who he is rejecting and what the consequences of his decision are.

"He uses that sickening joke that if he goes to hell all of his friends will be there so at least he won't be alone. He just doesn't care."

What lesson can be learned from this? Can a woman avoid being taken in by a man who says he is a Christian but isn't? There is no pat answer, but the fact that it can happen should serve as a warning that a woman must consider carefully whether the person she wants to marry is God's choice or her own.

We do know that God does not want one of His to marry out of the faith. So, if we make that assumption, then we must also trust that, if a woman truly is seeking God's will, He wants to reveal it to her. Certainly no one can assume that, because someone attends church and does religious things, that person is a Christian. Many women who married under these circumstances have told me that there were signs, but they ignored them because they were so much in love and so badly wanted to marry the man. Now, they are paying a price for their naiveté.

WHAT YOU DON'T KNOW CAN HURT YOU

A third way a woman becomes unequally yoked is to marry in ignorance. That was what happened in my case. I was raised in a Christian home and accepted the Lord when I was eight years old. But I came from a denomination in which baptism and salvation were synonymous. I was taught that you had to be baptized to be saved.

So, when I met George, I was more interested in his character assets and his personality than I was in anything to do with God. I truly believed that if we got married he could be baptized and that the act of immersion would secure him a place in heaven. I also thought that anyone who wasn't a Jew was a Christian.

We went to church together when we were engaged. He knew nothing about God, so he just went along with whatever I wanted in a religious sense. We were married in a Presbyterian church and I recall the pastor talking to us about the fact that we were joining in Christ and confirming with us that we were Christians. Evidently we both said all the right things. Although my parents were dead, my brothers, both of whom are believers, were quite pleased with my choice of a mate.

It wasn't until George and I had been married ten years and were on the brink of a divorce that God got hold of my life again and led me to a church where I heard the total truth of the salvation message. Three months after I totally surrendered my life to the Lord, George accepted Christ and we established our marriage, in a Christian sense, for the first time.

I am not saying God blesses ignorance, but I have to believe that our motives matter to Him. I operated on what I thought was true, on what loving parents and godly teachers had taught me. I didn't know my knowledge was incomplete and had no reason to question the accuracy of what I'd been told.

So, I was a Christian who married an unbeliever. No one had *ever* told me I should not marry someone who did not profess faith in Jesus Christ. And if anyone had, I would have explained that George was a Christian. He was honest, good, kind, stable, moral; and he promised he would be baptized.

I have met other women who also married in ignorance. Some of them don't have happy endings to their stories. I was very fortunate. God was exceedingly gracious to me. He did not punish me for my ignorance, which I could have corrected if I had been obedient in studying the Bible. I do not know why He was so merciful to me. I only know I feel obligated to do everything within my power to repay Him for His lovingkindness.

Since the only way to combat ignorance is with proper knowledge, this places a burden on Christians and the church to see that everyone in the body is taught God's command to not be unequally yoked.

We must teach this principle to young people so they can establish godly patterns for dating and selecting a mate. We have to teach it to parents so they can pass it on to their children and ingrain it into their early childhood instruction. An ounce of prevention is worth a lifetime of heartache.

I'LL WIN HIM LATER

The fourth, and final way, someone becomes unequally yoked is to willfully disobey God's direct command in 2 Corinthians 6:14-16: "Do not be bound together with unbelievers; for what partnership have righteousness and lawlessness, or what fellowship has light with darkness? Or what harmony has Christ with Belial, or what has a believer in common with an unbeliever? Or what agreement has the temple of God with idols? For we are the temple of the living God."

These verses consist of two parts. The first is the command to not be unequally yoked. Obviously, it is addressed to Christians. The second part deals with the rationale behind why it is sinful, even unthinkable, for a believer who belongs to God and is indwelt by the Holy Spirit, to link up with someone who belongs to Satan and is under his dominion.

To emphasize the impossibility of a believer uniting in a permanent relationship with an unbeliever, Paul asks several rhetorical questions. One is, "What partnership have righteousness and lawlessness?" He is referring to the fact of the believer's position in Christ. When we receive Christ we are made righteous in God's eyes. He accepts us because we are clothed in Christ's righteousness. It is, therefore, inconceivable that one who is in a position of perfection would attach herself to one who is totally sinful.

He also asks what fellowship light has with darkness. The Greek word for fellowship is *koinonia.* It implies an intimate relationship, a communion of souls. John tells us that "God is light, and in Him there is no darkness at all" (1 John 1:5). We are ordained to walk in the light and have fellowship with the Lord. If we unite with someone who is not walking in God's light, we are blocking His illumination in our lives, melding with the darkness of sin and choosing to live in the shadow of evil.

The next comparison is potent. Paul asks how Christ and the devil can have harmony. Obviously, they can't. When a believer marries an unbeliever, disharmony is a natural result. The disobedient Christian is intentionally joining a child of God to a child of Satan, forming an unholy alliance with the evil one, when in reality a Christian has already pledged herself to a holy union with the living God.

WHY GOD FORBIDS UNEQUAL YOKING

There are two primary reasons why God forbids the joining of a believer to an unbeliever. One is that Christians have been reborn; they are spiritually alive, whereas unbelievers are not. *A person who has not received Jesus Christ as personal Savior is spiritually dead!*

I shall never forget the time I heard a pastor explain that any regenerated sinner who joins with one who is not is like Doctor Frankenstein: creating a monster over which he eventually will lose control.

When a woman who is alive in Christ disobediently binds herself to an unbeliever, it is the same as amputating a leg from a corpse, then surgically attaching that dead, decaying appendage to her living body. The leg will never regenerate. Instead, it will cause infection and spread disease and poison throughout her entire being. And, she will have to live with the consequences of that action for the rest of her physical life.

The main reason God is against unequal yoking is that it is an affront to His holiness. God is separate and set apart from all that is sinful and evil. Those who belong to Him are to emulate His purity. God has commanded, "You shall be holy for I am holy" (Lev. 11:45).

Intermarriage reduces the purity factor in the life of the believer and adulterates the divine institution of marriage, which should be a reflection of the Christ-church relationship. Although, in His grace, God does not look upon the Christian wife or the children as defiled or impure, He must turn His back on the unbelieving mate, who abides in a permanent state of evil rather than in Him.

God cannot commune with the unsaved mate. Positionally he is unholy—unrighteous—because he has not been redeemed, so his sin is a barrier that walls him off from the presence and grace of God.

Not only is the purposeful joining of the believer to an unbeliever an affront to God's holiness, but the lifestyle of someone who is not a Christian also offends the Lord. During the time of the prophet Ezra the children of Israel had married outside of the faith. God's reaction was so pronounced that He demanded that every unbelieving mate be banished from the nation Israel.

Why did God react so strongly to this intermarriage? Ezra says it was because the unbelievers committed abominations against the Lord. What were the abominations? Worship of false gods and of idols, and participation in all of the paganism that was involved in the accompanying rituals.

If you trace what happens to God's children when they get involved with unbelievers, you will find drunkenness, murder, rape, incest, adultery, and desecration of the true worship procedures God has instituted. Reflect on David; what happened when he pursued Bathsheba?

You may recall that Solomon, who Scripture says is the wisest man who ever lived, foolishly brought heathen wives into the temple. This act almost destroyed him. He didn't do this when he was young and impetuous. He committed this sin when he was an old man. In his twilight years he was a broken man; depressed, despondent, and guilt-ridden, because he disobeyed God's law about intermarriage.

YOU REAP WHAT YOU SOW

How does God discipline a woman who has crossed this forbidden boundary; who has chosen to join the dead to the living, the holy to the unholy? Those whom I know and with whom I have talked say that basically they are reaping what they sowed. They live moment by moment with the results of their actions.

Constant ideological conflicts disrupt their marriage relationship. Their children are faced with the negative example of an ungodly father. Frequently, a woman is forced to choose between the Lord and the man she loves. She is plagued by the fact that her mate is not going to heaven and she cannot turn to the most important person in her life for spiritual guidance or counsel. She suffers oppression from living in the presence of evil.

But there is hope for the woman who is unequally yoked. She can rest with confidence in the fact that it is God's expressed will that He does not wish "for any to perish but for all to come to repentance" (2 Peter 3:9). So whether she was sovereignly placed in her position by God or attained her status as an unequally yoked wife because she was disobedient, she can depend on God's grace. He wants, more than she does, for her mate to come into the kingdom.

Some wives find solace in the fact that in the Book of Acts, when the jailer accepted Christ, Paul and Silas told him, "Believe in the Lord Jesus, and you shall be saved, you *and your household*" (Acts 16:31). Of course, this does not mean that her salvation guarantees that her husband and children will become Christians, but it strongly implies that her faith will act as a catalyst, bringing those she loves into union with God.

The woman who is unequally yoked will always be aware of the fact, but she must also remember that she is a child of God and a recipient of His magnificent love. Even if she married in total disobedience, that sin was paid for on the cross and the Lord wants her to live a fruitful, abundant life. She must cling to the positive blessing that she is the bride of Christ and is completely and perfectly loved by her Savior.

Workshop

1. Read Ezra 9:1-10:19, then answer the questions.
   a. What words are used to describe unbelievers?

   _____

   _____

   b. *Ezra 9:2.* What sin do the leaders confess?

   _____

   _____

   c. *Ezra 9:6.* What emotional reactions does Ezra have?

   _____

   _____

   d. *Ezra 9:12.* What impure motive underlies intermarriage?

   _____

   _____

   e. *Ezra 10:3-4.* Does the fact that God's law demanded that the foreigners be sent out mean that God condones divorce or that a woman who is unequally yoked can divorce her husband for that reason? (See 1 Corinthians 7:12-13 for answer.)

   _____

   _____

2. Look up each "hope" verse, then answer the question.
   a. *Psalms 39:7; 71:5.* Where can an unequally yoked wife find hope?

   _____

   _____

   b. *Psalm 43:5.* What will defeat depression?

   _____

   _____

   c. *Proverbs 10:28; Jeremiah 17:7.* What by-product of hope is named in these verses?

   _____

   _____

   d. *Lamentations 3:26 (KJV).* This statement is perfect advice for one who is unequally yoked. What two things does it say a person should do?

   _____

   _____

   e. *Romans 8:24-25.* According to the concept in these verses, should a wife who is hoping her mate will come to Christ expect to see outward evidence? Why or why not?

   _____

   _____

   What should her approach be?

   _____

   _____

   _____

Being a Suitable Helper

It appears that one of the biggest problems an unequally yoked wife faces is that she believes she is different from other Christian wives. She is hurtfully aware of how many church activities are planned for couples. She's the one whose husband won't come with her to the Wednesday night potluck, the Christmas cantata, or the Sunday school program. She can't pray or read the Bible with him. She sees herself as an exception, rather than a rule, so dwells on how different her marriage is.

Perhaps those of us who are married in the faith perpetuate this myth; somehow we mirror the idea that every event in our lives, from mopping floors to buying a new car, happens on some sort of super-spiritual level, when in reality Christian couples also have differences. They fight. They don't always believe alike or agree on how to raise the kids, how much money to give to the church, or where to go on vacation.

Christian husbands come home from work tired and frustrated. They lose their tempers. They yell at the kids. They don't always pray with their wives when they are distressed, nor do they conduct nightly devotions with wisdom and wit. Christian husbands and wives are just as human, and sometimes as carnal, as unbelievers are.

As a result of this misconception, the unequally yoked wife tends to "idealize" Christian marriage and possibly blame many normal marriage problems on the fact that her husband is an unbeliever. She is positive that if her husband came to Christ her marriage would be blissful and almost problem free. Each of the women I interviewed for this book said that although she intellectually knows all marriages have pitfalls and problems, she has (or had) the unrealistic expectation that if her husband would accept Christ, her marriage would become one of the "made in heaven" variety.

Because an unequally yoked marriage lacks the spiritual quality that Christian marriages have, she may even become jealous of her sisters who are married to believers. She may silently play a game called, "If only he was a Christian," which makes it more difficult for her to be a good wife or to be satisfied and enjoy her marriage.

Constance observed that, "We all go through a time when our identity is 'me, with the unsaved husband.' And we wish so badly he was a Christian. But eventually God shows us that our identity is with Him and we stand or fall by our position in Christ, not on the fact of our husband's salvation."

Tammy explained her feelings this way: "I have always idealized thoughts of a Christian marriage, to the point where I was envious of women who are married to believers. I have realized this is wrong. One day I thought, what if God said, 'Tammy, Rod is never going to commit his life to Me. Now, what are you going to do about your marriage?'"

She continued, "One thing is sure, I couldn't sit around waiting for him to be saved. God showed me that our happiness cannot depend on whether he comes to Christ. Facing that made me look at myself and see that I was not the wife God wanted me to be. Now, I am freer. It is easier to enjoy being with Rod because I don't think of him as my unsaved husband but as the man I love, with whom I will spend the rest of my natural life. What happens in eternity is in God's hands."

Tammy has learned what each unequally yoked wife must: that

in God's eyes a wife is a wife is a wife, regardless of the status of her husband. The Lord has assigned specific roles and duties for all wives, whether they are married to believers or unbelievers. If an unequally yoked wife understands her role and what God expects from her, she can minister to her husband more effectively and have a transforming impact on his life.

WHAT IT MEANS TO BE A HELPMEET (HELPER)

Basically, God wants an unequally yoked wife to be what He wants any Christian wife to be—a godly, loving companion to her husband. Physically, the Lord created man before He created woman. He fellowshiped with Adam in the Garden and gave him work to do. But the Lord God knew He had one more thing to do before Paradise was complete. He said, "It is not good for the man to be alone; I will make him a helper suitable for him" (Gen. 2:18), thereby establishing a wife's primary role: that of being a helpmeet to her husband.

The word "helpmeet" or "helper" contains many subtle meanings. A key meaning is the idea of suitability. The Amplified Bible reads, "I will make him a helper meet (suitable, adapted, completing) for him." A wife is fashioned by God, both in her physical and emotional make-up, to be complementary to her husband: to adapt to and complete him.

She is the balancing component in his life. Where he is weak, she is strong; where he lacks sensitivity, she is tender; where he is vulnerable, she is firm. And because a husband/wife team is structured to enhance each other's good points and supplement each other in areas of weakness, a wife can be her husband's greatest asset and aid. She can be used by God in unique, exciting, creative ways because she is suited to help him.

The word "helper" is the same word that is used elsewhere in Scripture to illustrate that God is our helper—our strength, guide, and undergirder. This is not a passive position but a vital, active, dynamic one. And just as Eve was created for Adam, to fulfill and complete his life, each wife was chosen and ordained by God for her particular husband. She is suitable for him, so she can have a special ministry to him and contribute to his life in ways that no one else can. She was made to assist and accompany him. The Lord will use her to nurture her husband intellectually, emotionally, and spiritually, if she is willing.

Simply put, a wife is to be the same kind of helper to her husband that God is to His bride, the church! This dynamic duty embodies several elements. One is the idea of protection. God is "our help and our shield" (Ps. 33:20), so as a helpmeet, a wife is responsible for assisting and shielding her husband.

This runs contrary to our cultural concept of the man protecting the woman, doesn't it? Yet, any wife knows that there are many ways in which she shields her husband. She may guard him from unnecessary problems, set a peaceful atmosphere in the home, and do whatever she can to alleviate stress in his life. She protects his health by cooking the right kinds of foods and should be concerned for both his physical and spiritual well-being. At times, when appropriate, she will shelter him from situations that will hurt him. She takes care of him and ministers to his needs by doing things for him that will make his life easier.

A GOOD HELPMEET IS FAITHFUL

Ministering in this capacity also involves a foundational element called trust. God, our role model, is a faithful helper. Scripture proclaims, "Great is Thy faithfulness" (Lam. 3:23). The Lord isn't just a little bit trustworthy. His faithfulness is expansive, deep, immense, overwhelming! He never lets us down. He is always there when we need Him, so much so that He acts on our behalf even when we are not aware He is intervening. A wife who is a true helpmeet will be there for her husband in the same way. He will know he can always, under any circumstances, depend on her.

A godly wife will manifest the kind of fidelity that allows "the heart of her husband [to trust] in her" (Prov. 31:11). Her husband will know he can rely on her with his total being, certain that, "She [will do] him good and not evil all the days of her life" (Prov. 31:12).

A wife who emulates God in her role as helper has a faith that endures; a total, permanent commitment to her husband that lasts throughout the marriage. She "bears all things, believes all things, hopes all things, endures all things" (1 Cor. 13:7).

A GOOD HELPMEET IS A COUNSELOR

Another component of being a suitable helper is that of counselor; being a sounding board and a resource person of inestimable value. This is an area where many Christian wives experience confusion. They mistakenly believe that it is not submissive to give advice to their husbands, to share ideas and opinions, to make suggestions, or to differ with them. God is our counselor. David noted, "With Thy counsel Thou wilt guide me" (Ps. 73:24). Likewise, God uses a wife's counsel to guide her husband.

In a marriage, where two are one flesh, what one partner does affects the other. It is especially important in an unequally yoked marriage, where the unbeliever does not have any other source for the counsel of the Lord except his wife, that she incorporate scriptural ideals and principles into their lifestyle by the advice she offers and the values she maintains.

When Winifred and I met for coffee, she was so frustrated she was on the verge of tears. "Sam wants to take all the money we've saved for the down payment on a house and buy a boat, a stupid twelve thousand dollar boat!" Obviously, she was angry. I knew she had kept her job and delayed having children so they could save the cash for a home. No wonder she was upset.

I asked the inevitable question: "What was Sam's reaction when he saw how upset you are and when you told him you wouldn't go along with buying a boat with the house money?"

She dabbed at her eyes with a tissue and said, "I didn't say anything." She went on to explain that she was afraid to say something, for fear she would be breaking God's command to "be submissive to your own husbands so that even if any of them are disobedient to the word, they may be won without a word by the behavior of their wives" (1 Peter 3:1).

We spent the next one-and-one-half hours talking about the balance between submission and passivity. When she left she was confident she could make her husband see how foolish it would be to buy the boat, in light of the long range effect it would have on their lives. They wanted a home and children, and Winifred wasn't willing to sacrifice those for a water sport.

She called later to tell me that Sam had been quite reasonable once she started communicating with him. But what if she hadn't performed her role as counselor? She'd be nursing anger, bitterness, and resentment. And they wouldn't be the proud owners of a new house. Mainly, she would have done them both a disservice by not speaking out.

Unequally yoked wives tell me they frequently feel they don't have much influence over their husbands; that what they say and think doesn't matter. I don't believe that. I think the problem is that they do not know how to communicate. They are afraid they'll leave their Christianity open to criticism if they take a firm stand or advise their husbands. Open, honest communication is essential to any marriage, regardless of the spiritual standing of either party. Instead of forsaking her position as counselor, the unequally yoked wife needs to learn how to properly communicate her ideas and to be such a wise and loving resource person that her husband will come to rely on her advice and opinions.

A GOOD HELPMEET IS A COMPANION

Along with helpmeet, another wifely role mentioned in Genesis 2:18 (LB) is that of companion.

God noted that it is not good for man to be alone. He wanted man to understand that too, so He did an interesting thing. After He determined He would "make a helper suitable for him" (Gen. 2:18), He didn't immediately make woman. Instead, He made the lower animals and birds, then brought them to Adam so he could name them. And after Adam had named all of the beasts of the field and birds of the sky, he realized that among all those creatures there wasn't one that was suitable to be his companion;

one who was complementary to him, with whom he could have fellowship.

I think the Lord God chose that way to show man that he is incomplete without woman; that no other living creature can fulfill his needs the way she can. Adam needed a wife—a companion and friend—so he would not be lonely, but would have someone with whom to share his life.

The unequally yoked wife must be careful not to neglect this aspect of her marriage relationship. Many have told me that they would rather talk to and be with their Christian friends than their husbands, because those friends understand things their husbands can't. While that may be true, there are many non-spiritual things wives can share with their husbands.

Rene and Andy have been married for thirty-two years. They golf together, play tennis, go to the theater and ballet. They travel a lot. They have a wide circle of friends and generally enjoy each other and their life together. They are what I would call a close, loving couple.

Rene is a Christian and Andy is not. She accepted the Lord when they had been married eight years. When I asked her how she had managed to gain such a balance in her life, she told me she decided that the only thing she and her husband did not have in common was Christ, but that she was going to share every other area of her life with him.

"I loved him when I married him. His zest for life and his diverse interests were what attracted me to him in the first place. I don't think God wants to interfere with our relationship, but make it better. And, He has." Rene is a lady who knows how to be a friend and companion to her husband.

Solomon, in describing what a friend is, said he or she is someone who "loves at all times" (Prov. 17:17) and "sticks closer than a brother" (Prov. 18:24). Jesus noted that the ultimate act of friendship is a willingness to sacrifice self. "Greater love has no one than this, that one lay down his life for his friends" (John 15:13). Part of a wife's role is to be that kind of friend to the man she married.

A GOOD HELPMEET IS A WILLING SEXUAL PARTNER

Beyond companionship, a wife is to be a willing sexual partner for her husband. This part of the relationship is not to be maintained out of duty or obligation, but out of love and desire. God told Eve, "You shall bring forth children; yet your desire shall be for your husband" (Gen. 3:16). It is normal for a wife to want a physical relationship with her husband. This is true whether or not he is a believer.

Several years ago, when I was taping a Bible course called, "Sex Within Marriage: God's View," I asked the women to submit their questions in writing. One of the most pertinent was turned in by an unequally yoked wife who said, "I'm married to an unbeliever. Neither of us were Christians when we were married. I came to Christ and my husband hasn't. Although I love him very much, I feel guilty every time we have intercourse because I'm plagued by the idea that I'm joining a child of Satan with a child of God. This has really decreased my enjoyment. What should I do?"

I'm sure that other women in her position may feel the same way. A look into God's Word should alleviate their anxiety. First, we find that God thought up the idea of sex: "male and female He created them" (Gen. 1:27). Then He divinely and sovereignly instituted marriage. He physically formed woman from the man, then had them unite in a one-flesh relationship. Sexual intercourse sealed the marriage commitment. And it must have been a natural act because "the man and his wife were both naked and were not ashamed" (Gen. 2:25). So not only is sex God-created but it is God-ordained within a marriage.

The apostle Paul taught, while dealing specifically with the unequally yoked situation, that God does not view sexual intercourse between a Christian and his or her unbelieving mate as joining a child of God with a child of Satan. Instead, in His grace He sees it as sanctified—pure and holy—because one of His children is involved.

When a Christian woman is married to an unbeliever, that marriage is looked upon by God as set apart and separate from the world. In His eyes, the union with an unbeliever is still godly and holy. The marriage is clothed in Christ's righteousness because the believer is. The marriage is sanctified and the husband lives in the presence of the Holy Spirit, who is at work in the life of the believing wife. Because of this, the unequally yoked wife is completely free to enjoy a full, meaningful sexual relationship with her husband. She can rest on the promise that God looks upon their children with favor and blessing. "The unbelieving husband is sanctified through his wife . . . for otherwise your children are unclean, but now they are holy" (1 Cor. 7:14).

A GOOD HELPMEET MAKES HIM PROUD

Within the basic role of helper and of being a friend and lover to her husband, a wife is faced with multitudes of responsibilities. One is that she will please her husband. Proverbs 12:4 observes, "An excellent wife is the crown of her husband, but she who shames him is as rottenness in his bones."

A wife is always on display as part of her husband's identity. She is "Mrs." He "wears" her as a ruler would a crown. She is an obvious, noticeable, highly visible part of his life. And every man wants to be able to point to his wife with pride.

Unbelieving husbands, however, tell me that they are sometimes ashamed of their Christian wives because they are so critical, if not in words then in attitude, of everything they do, of their friends, and of the places they go. They are embarrassed by their wives' "religion," and as difficult as it may be to accept, that is a legitimate complaint. Unbelieving husbands are afraid their wives will come off as fanatics, as "holier than thou," to people they care about.

One man told me his wife was always outwardly pleasant to his friends. Although she didn't talk to them much, she was cordial. But, he said, "When we're working on the car or playing cards, and she brings us sandwiches and beer, she slams them onto the table or acts as if her hands are dirty because she touched a beer bottle." This embarrasses him, but when he tried to explain to his wife how her attitude was coming across, she (in his words) "lectured me on the evils of drinking." And he couldn't understand why she had to make such a big deal about a couple of drinks.

He found a way to solve the problem. He and his friends just go somewhere else because, "I don't feel welcome in my own home when I'm doing certain things my wife disapproves of."

A wife, any wife, is to be a crown to her husband, and if an unequally yoked wife makes major issues out of minor ones, she will drive her husband from her *and* from the Lord. Regardless of her own standards, she must be extremely careful not to embarrass him or put him down. She needs to remember that Christ, who is her example, was always right out there among the drinkers, gluttons, prostitutes, and sinners. That was how He reached them with His love. She has to learn how to show her disapproval without being condemning or judgmental. She must try to be such a great wife that her unbelieving husband can point to her as "an excellent wife."

A GOOD HELPMEET DOES THINGS GOD'S WAY

She won't be able to do this if her attitude is not right; if she is silently critical or acts as if she is "better" than her unsaved husband and his associates. It's a fact of life that we convey our feelings through our actions more than by what we say. So the unequally yoked wife must exercise special care not to play the martyr; not to come across as if her marriage is a cross she has to bear for the Lord's sake. Any negative attitudes will show, so she needs to cultivate positive, godly thoughts that will shine from her countenance.

Frequently we look at the virtuous woman in Proverbs 31 from the standpoint of her performance, but the more I read and dwell on that passage, the more I am struck by her attitude. She's a nice person who enjoys life and is fun to be around. For instance, she's a cheerful doer. "She works with her hands in delight" (Prov. 31:13).

Cindy, a vivacious young wife who came to Christ two weeks after she was married, shared that to her this means she sings while she dumps her husband's ashtrays and doesn't crab about buying liquor for him when she grocery shops.

This excellent wife in Proverbs 31 is also excited about being a wife. She's industrious and energetic and does everything wholeheartedly. But the thing that stands out the most about her is that she has a pleasant disposition. "She opens her mouth in wisdom, and the teaching of kindness is on her tongue" (Prov. 31:26). She isn't so distracted by what she's doing that she yells at the kids and nags her husband. She is happy and content. "She senses that her gain is good; and she smiles at the future" (Prov. 31:18, 25).

She doesn't go around talking about what a godly woman she is. She *lives* her faith and lets "her works praise her in the gates" (Prov. 31:31). And her husband is her biggest fan! He praises her publicly when he sits with the elders in the city gates. He thinks she's the best wife who ever lived, and he tells her so. "Many daughters have done nobly, but you excel them all" (Prov. 31:29). What wife wouldn't want to hear those words?

Interestingly, we are not told anything about her husband's faith or his spiritual status. But we see that because she was the kind of woman God wanted her to be, she had a happy home and a contented, loving husband.

Our homes are where we live. An unequally yoked wife can have immeasurable influence there. If she is wise, she will take advantage of her domestic setting and use it as a womb in which the Lord can woo and win her husband into birth in God's kingdom. She can use their home and her God-given position as a wife to counterbalance the worldliness that predominates her husband's life. She must be open to the wonder of their love. She must devote herself to him, the same as she would if he were the greatest Christian who ever lived.

She needs to learn to separate her personal reactions to what her husband does from the actual agitation of the Holy Spirit. And above all, she must do everything within her power to be the kind of helper, friend, and counselor to her unbelieving husband that God meant her to be.

Workshop

1. Look up each verse and write what it teaches about an un-equally yoked wife's *attitude* toward her unbelieving husband.

   a. *1 Corinthians 10:31.* _____

   _____

   b. *Philippians 4:11.* _____

   _____

   c. *1 Thessalonians 5:16.* _____

   _____

   d. *James 4:10.* _____

   _____

   e. *1 Peter 3:15.* _____

   _____

2. Look up each verse and write what it teaches about an un-equally yoked wife's *actions* toward her unbelieving husband.

   a. *Psalm 37:8.* _____

   _____

   b. *Psalm 130:4.* _____

   _____

c. *Proverbs 18:13.* _____

_____

d. *1 Corinthians 9:19.* _____

_____

e. *Galatians 6:2.* _____

_____

3. Read each of these statements, then check the response you think your *husband* would make.

	Always	Usually	Some-times	Never
a. I can rely on my wife to help, even without my asking.				
b. My wife is emotionally supportive.				
c. When my wife disagrees with me, she is not angry or judgmental.				
d. I value my wife's opinions.				
e. My wife does whatever is within her power to create a peaceful atmosphere in our home.				

	Always	Usually	Some-times	Never
f. I totally trust my wife.				
g. My wife has my welfare in mind when we are making decisions.				
h. My wife and I have fun to-gether.				
i. Our sexual relationship is important and satisfying to my wife.				
j. I am proud of my wife.				

Now, read the statements to your husband and mark his responses. How do his responses compare with yours?

In areas where there is a marked difference, what can you do to make the necessary changes?

Being a First-Peter-Three Partner

Although being a helpmeet is a wife's primary responsibility, there are many variances in the way that role is implemented. The situation of an unequally yoked wife differs from that of women who are married to Christians. So God has given her a basic principle of action which, if adhered to, enables her to be used as a constructive instrument in her husband's life.

That principle is found in 1 Peter 3:1-4. "You wives, be submissive to your own husbands so that even if any of them are disobedient to the word, they may be won *without a word* by the behavior of their wives, as they observe your chaste and respectful behavior. And let not your adornment be external only—braiding the hair and wearing gold jewelry, and putting on dresses; but let it be the hidden person of the heart, with the imperishable quality of a gentle and quiet spirit, which is precious in the sight of God."

In His grace, the Lord lovingly gave those instructions. While there is no panacea, no simple solution to the multitude of dilemmas these unequally yoked women face, it includes a positive plan of action.

It offers the hope that if a Christian wife is obedient, she may win her husband to the Lord through the example of her godly behavior. It tells her how to be a First-Peter-Three Partner.

While this imposition of silence is difficult, St. Gregory wisely observed, "It is needful that we sometimes endure, keeping to ourselves what evil men are, in order that they may learn in us, by our good living, what they are not." That is a perfect description of the responsibility of the unequally yoked wife.

God's formula contains a positive approach to the marriage —be submissive—and wields some common sense advice on what not to do: Do not try to talk an unsaved husband to the Lord. God has good reasons for imposing such a stringent restriction. One is that it is so easy to say one thing and be another. If a wife tries to "preach" her husband to Christ while she is failing by example, she will only alienate him further.

Also, if she tries to point out his sin to him, she will create unbearable friction in their marriage. All unsaved people hate to be told about their sin. It causes a terrible dilemma for them. If they deny it, they look foolish, because sin is so obvious. If they admit it, they also are admitting they need to be saved from it, or that they should take steps to correct what they are doing. Saying, "I am a sinner," is the first overture of repentance that leads to the cross.

So, if a woman verbally accuses her husband of his sin, she puts him in an impossible situation. She will cause dissension in her home. And, chances are her husband will not listen to her, but will retaliate with a few instances of her imperfections which he would like to see eliminated.

Also, verbalizing won't work because it is impossible to communicate spiritual truth to an unspiritual person. It is like trying to carry on a conversation with a baby who is still in the womb, who hasn't yet been born. That infant can't relate to what is said nor understand the content of the message. The same is true with a person who has not been born spiritually. Nagging, lecturing, or explaining will not bring a person to the Lord, because "the natural, nonspiritual man does not accept or welcome or admit into his heart the gifts and teachings and revelations of the Spirit of God, for they are folly (meaningless nonsense) to him; and he is *incapable* of knowing them" (1 Cor. 2:14 Amplified).

The unequally yoked wife must understand this, not just with her intellect, but with her heart. *Nothing she says about God will make her husband love the Lord or want to turn his life over to Him.* Regeneration is an act of the Holy Spirit. God uses people to bring about that process, but only if they do what He has instructed. He has told women who are unequally yoked not to try to communicate verbally about spiritual things with their unbelieving mates. The problem in following this principle is in deciding how to practice it so one can be used as God's silent instrument of salvation.

MARRIAGE IS A PARTNERSHIP

If a Christian wife is effectively to act out this principle, she needs to grasp the full meaning of what marriage is, and what submission is and is not. Too many unequally yoked wives place an unfair burden on themselves because they do not understand that their marriages are no different from all other marriages except in the way they are to handle spiritual matters. Marriage is a partnership, regardless of the spiritual state of either person. But in an unequal matching, the believing wife must separate the spiritual from the secular aspects of the relationship.

The Lord has commanded that she *not* communicate with her husband. This means she is not to communicate about the things of God. In all other matters, she is free, as a marriage partner, to share her feelings and opinions and to advise her husband.

She must not confuse cultural standards with biblical ones. Lifestyle issues—such as who changes diapers, who mows the lawn, who mops the floor, should a wife be employed outside of her home, decisions about how money is spent, what color to paint the walls, and where to go on vacation—are not spiritual issues. These kinds of things should be decided by each couple, based on what they believe is best for their marriage, within the framework of their own personalities and family structure.

Yet, many unequally yoked wives I interviewed told me they always give in to their unbelieving husbands, even in secular matters where they disagree, because they do not want to be non-submissive. In actuality, by withholding vital communication they are failing in their role as helper, counselor, and companion.

Of course, there will be times when a delicate balance exists between submission and non-submission, so it is imperative that the unequally yoked wife fathom what submission is and what it is not, so she can draw the necessary distinctions between when to give in and when to stand her ground.

WHAT SUBMISSION IS AND IS NOT

Most importantly, she must understand that submission is not blind obedience, although obedience is sometimes a by-product of submission. Whereas obedience is following orders, submission is voluntarily surrendering or yielding the will. In Scripture, wives are exhorted to submit or subject themselves to their husbands. Children are told to obey. (See Col. 3:18, 20 and Eph. 5:22; 6:1.) And there is a vast difference between the role of a wife and that of a child. Obedience doesn't leave room for choice; submission does.

Phyllis is a woman who, in her desire to please the Lord and win her husband, almost ruined her marriage because she didn't comprehend the difference between obedience and submission. She and Don had been married over six years when she accepted Christ. She is an outgoing, fun-loving, spunky person and Dan loves her wit and her independent spirit. She told me that he is always telling her one of the things he appreciates most about her is that she is a capable, self-sufficient person, "and that he can't stand women who are clinging vines."

Immediately after Phyllis came to the Lord she started attending a women's Bible study. The topic was submission, and somehow she got a limited perspective about it. She wanted to have a gentle and quiet spirit, so she stopped discussing things with Dan, the way she had prior to her conversion, and didn't clown around as much. No matter what he suggested, she smiled and agreed. She was miserable, because she was squelching her personality, and Dan was "on her case" all the time, asking if she was mad at him or not feeling well.

Finally, one night, just to see if he could get a normal reaction from her, he told her that he'd been offered a transfer and that they were going to move to Alaska. Submissive wife that she'd become, she gulped back tears, seethed inside and nodded. Dan blew! He accused her of not loving him any more and not caring what happened in their lives. He screamed that she had changed so much it was like living with a stranger. Phyllis burst into tears and tried to explain that she was just trying to be a good wife. Her husband's reply was, "Well, if this is what God does for you, who wants Him?"

The next day she went to her pastor for counsel and he was able to clarify her misconceptions. He invited her and Dan to go with him and his family to a baseball game. He made Phyllis promise not to mention the Lord all evening, to enjoy the game the way she always did.

That was three years ago. Dan still hasn't accepted Christ, but he sometimes goes to church with Phyllis and is open to being friends with Christians. And she has returned to her outgoing, sparkling self. She learned the hard way that submission and obedience are not synonymous.

SUBMISSION IS FOR ALL CHRISTIANS

Another misjudgment is that submission is "for women only." It is not. Submission is an attitude of a Christ-centered life. It is humility in practice; compliance to the leading of the Holy Spirit. The Bible teaches that children are to submit to parents, citizens to government, young men and Christians to their leaders, and ultimately, we are all to "be subject to one another in the fear of Christ" (Eph. 5:21).

All of us in the family of God are to, "do nothing from selfishness or empty conceit, but with humility of mind let each of you regard one another as more important than himself; do not merely look out for your own personal interests, but also for the interests of others" (Phil. 2:3-4).

We are to be unselfishly submissive.

Submission, then, is a non-resistant attitude that counters selfishness of the flesh and is exemplified to us by God's Son, "who, although He existed in the form of God, did not regard equality with God a thing to be grasped" (Phil. 2:6).

God, in His wisdom, chose to institute a universal principle of order in the marriage relationship, so He ordained that "Christ is the head of every man, and the [husband] is the head of a [wife], and God is the head of Christ" (1 Cor. 11:3). This is accomplished when "wives [are] subject to [their] own husbands, as to the Lord" (Eph. 5:22). That is God's divine blueprint for the structuring of the marriage partnership. So true submission means a wife will acknowledge her place in God's order, voluntarily acquiesce to her husband's leadership, and trust that the Lord will use him as a directing factor in her life.

This principle applies whether or not the husband is saved. The husband is the head of his wife, period. Yet too many unequally yoked wives think that God is limited because their husbands are not Christians. If they are wise, they will use his God-given position to their advantage.

Susie learned that the hard way. She was quite distraught when she came to see me. She had inherited some property prior to her marriage and now had to decide whether or not to sell it. She was employed, so she used part of her income for upkeep and taxes. The property was becoming a financial burden to her, but the land had been in the family for generations and she hated to sell it.

She told me she had prayed and had asked a Christian attorney, Christian friends, and her Sunday school teacher what she should do, but had received conflicting counsel. "I simply don't know what to do," she confessed.

My first question was, "What does your husband think you should do?"

She looked surprised. "I don't know. I haven't shared the problem with him. He isn't a Christian and I wanted godly counsel, so I didn't ask his advice."

As we searched the Scriptures, she realized that God was not limited in the way He could use her husband. She immediately asked him what he thought she should do and was relieved when he took over the matter. He lifted the burden of the decision from her. He came up with a plan so that she not only kept her inheritance but turned it into income property.

Susie learned that she dare not shut out her husband from any facet of her life. The unequally yoked wife must respect her spouse's position as God's representative authority, trusting that He will work through her husband to accomplish His will in her life and marriage.

An unequally yoked wife can rest assured that God can and will use her unbelieving husband to direct her. He can formulate His desires through her mate. God is not limited because her husband doesn't believe.

THE FIRST-PETER-THREE PRINCIPLE

First Peter 3:1-4 tells what an unequally yoked wife must do so God can use her husband as a guiding element in her life, and so she, in turn, can be used by the Lord to draw her husband to Christ. God has given her a positive approach to the spiritual aspects of both her marriage and her own Christianity; the "how to's" of being a godly wife in such unique, and sometimes trying circumstances.

First, wives are told, "Be submissive to your own husbands so that even if any of them are disobedient to the word, they may be won without a word by the behavior of their wives" (1 Peter 3:1). Once again, the pages of God's Holy Word emphasize a proven truth: that actions speak louder than words. Her unbelieving husband will be won, not by what she says, but "as [he observes her] chaste and respectful behavior" (1 Peter 3:2). Since words come easily, but the sifting away of sinful behavior is a slow, tedious process, a wife would be apt to say one thing while being another. So the Lord imposed this restriction to protect Himself and the Christian wife from scorn and ridicule.

No one knows us better than our families. They're there when we lose our tempers, show our true feelings; when we let it all hang out. They know our weaknesses and our sin patterns. So if a Christian wife verbally shares her faith with her unbelieving husband and tells him what God's standards are and what changes he should make in his attitude and actions, she had better be ready to live up to those requirements herself. But because she still has that Old Sin Nature, because she is as human as the next person, she cannot. So, if she talks her faith, she can fail by example and disgrace both herself and the Lord.

To keep this from happening, God reverses the pattern. He instructs the unequally yoked wife to change her behavior, and as He transforms her into the image of Christ, her husband will *see* what God is like and her acted-out faith will convince him of the validity of her Christianity. But, while she is growing, if she backslides or blows her witness, her mate won't have grounds for judging, condemning, or harrassing her.

ACTIONS SPEAK LOUDER THAN WORDS

Next, Paul defines how the unequally yoked wife should act. She is to be chaste. That's a rather old-fashioned sounding word that means pure. Ruth shared what this means to her: that she must never let down on her standards or live in opposition to stated scriptural principles. "I always have to maintain the difference between Christianity and the world, and by example, show my husband how God's way is best.

"But," she cautioned, "being chaste does not mean being prudish or holier than thou. It means being godly, Spirit-filled."

It also means the unbelieving husband can trust his wife; that she will be loyal and devoted to him. She will be sexually monogamous and mentally faithful, not wishing he was other than who he is. (Most unsaved husbands are keenly aware that their wives wish they were Christians.)

It means her husband can expect his wife to speak favorably of him and hold him up in a complimentary light to her Christian friends. Chastity involves a total commitment to the marriage partner's welfare.

The unequally yoked wife also is to be respectful, to honor her husband's position and him as a person. I am sure that sometimes this is hard, especially if the husband is extremely worldly, but it is a command from the Lord. Several unequally yoked women told me that they cannot respect their husbands because they aren't saved. The wives are guilty of a sort of spiritual pride and tend to look down on their mates as less than worthy of respect because of this.

Others said they concentrate too much on their husbands' negative qualities, rather than their good ones (something all wives do at one time or another), and have to make a conscious effort to dwell on the positives which deserve respect.

The godly woman in Proverbs "does [her husband] good and not evil all the days of her life" (Prov. 31:12). Sometimes wives do irreparable damage to their husbands' reputations by the way they speak of them. I know there have been many instances when unequally yoked wives have portrayed, in their prayer requests, what deplorable people their husbands are. As others listen, they draw conclusions and often form wrong or unfair opinions. Respecting her husband means she will not downgrade him in the eyes of others, in any way.

It also means she will hold him in esteem personally. If a Christian woman cannot respect her unbelieving husband's words and worldly habits, at least she can honor him as her husband; as the man she married for better or worse. She can dignify the relationship about its circumstances by venerating his "office" in her life.

Too often unbelieving husbands are treated like second-class citizens. Diane confessed to me that she had been guilty of this attitude. She had what she called a "spiritual superiority" complex. She wasn't aware of it at the time, but she mentally put down her husband. She mocked his ideas and his reactions or responses and secretly made fun of his opinions.

Finally, one day, when she visited him at his office, she was struck by the tremendous respect his co-workers, his secretary, and his boss showed him. She shared how she got a knot in her stomach when she heard a man who is older and more experienced than her husband say, "Yes, sir," to him. And she was both frightened and ashamed when she saw how his young secretary looked up to and admired him.

"She came into the office with coffee for us and when John thanked her she didn't just say 'You're welcome.' She said, 'Is there anything else I can get for you? Anything you need?'"

Diane confided, "When I got to the car, I started crying. I was so ashamed. I hated myself. I thought about how sweet John is, and how handsome and appealing as a person. I spent the next three days praying and confessing my disrespectful attitude. John asked me if there was anything wrong and I told him I would talk with him about it when I was able to cope. He was so kind to me, without even knowing why I was hurting. And when I asked his forgiveness, he was upset that I was being too hard on myself.

"The thing that disturbed me most," she continued, "is that I was judging him not because of his actions or because he isn't a good husband, but because he wasn't what I wanted him to be. I was disrespectful to him because he isn't a Christian." Diane knows now that the best way a wife can show her unbelieving husband that God loves him is to treat him with esteem.

EMULATING A GENTLE, QUIET SPIRIT

Finally, the unequally yoked wife is to manifest the fruit of the Spirit. Rather than concentrating on outward beauty, she is told, "Let not your adornment be external only—braiding the hair, and wearing gold jewelry, and putting on dresses" (1 Peter 3:3). This doesn't mean she isn't supposed to dress nicely or make herself attractive, but that she should cultivate "the hidden person of the heart," concentrating on "the imperishable quality of a gentle and quiet spirit, which is precious in the sight of God" (1 Peter 3:4).

The meaning of "gentle and quiet spirit" is frequently misunderstood. The word *quiet*, as it is used in this passage, doesn't mean lack of noise or activity, but lack of agitation or harshness. It doesn't mean a godly woman is to be passive, complacent, or speak in a whisper. It doesn't mean she can't differ with her husband or that she has to be withdrawn or uncommunicative. It means she is to cultivate the peace of God in her life.

It won't be easy, but an unequally yoked wife is not supposed to worry about her husband's salvation. Instead, she has to leave him in God's hands, because if she doesn't, she'll try to convert him with words rather than actions. She mustn't be anxious about what is going to happen to him or their marriage. She is to concentrate on being the best wife she possibly can, loving and respecting her husband, enjoying their relationship, and leaving the results to God. When she does, she will not be "frightened by any fear" (1 Peter 3:6).

PRAYING PROPERLY

Although it sounds difficult, many Christian women have been able to develop into First-Peter-Three wives. I asked some of them if they could share with their sisters who are unequally yoked one great gem of advice or wisdom concerning how this could best be accomplished. Their answers offer practical insight on how to implement God's instruction to win their husbands without a word.

Prayer topped everyone's list. We will discuss this in detail in another chapter, but every unequally yoked woman said that praying for her husband gave her a different perspective about him and their marriage. "And I don't mean asking God to save him or change him into what I want him to be," Betty stressed, "but asking the Lord to bless him and use me to make him happy, to meet his needs, and to be the completer of his faith. I mean thanking God for him and our marriage and asking for more love for him every day."

LONGSUFFERING SOMETIMES MEANS SUFFERING LONG

A majority of the unequally yoked wives said they wished there was some way they could warn their sisters in Christ, who are in similar situations, to be patient with the results of their husbands' unbelief. Sara wisely noted, "Sure, Tom swears sometimes and he doesn't see why I think it's so wrong to cheat on our income tax, but I lose my temper and get very judgmental. Those are sins, too, only I should know better because God sets my moral standards. Tom has to come up with his own."

She cautioned that unequally yoked wives need to be sure that what they are angry or impatient about is not their husbands' lack of spirituality. "I know sometimes I get bent out of shape about dirty socks in the middle of the floor or the fact that he didn't put out the trash, but inside my head I'm thinking, if only he was a Christian, things like this wouldn't happen. I camouflage my resentment by being impatient about other things."

These women stressed the danger of dwelling on the fact that a husband is not saved. They expressed the concern that when this happens, they automatically want to try to convert their mates by talking to them about the Lord, rather than by living the example. Denise feels that, "Many of us are negative instead of positive about our situations. We are defeated and act as if our husbands are a lost cause. Instead, we need to develop a gentle and quiet spirit by clinging to God's promises in hope! I know my negative attitudes come through as if I was wearing a sign. Ed can tell when I am down on him because he isn't Joe Christian."

Other practical suggestions these unequally yoked wives shared about implementing the First-Peter-Three principle are:

1. Remember, you take the Holy Spirit with you wherever you go. Don't avoid social functions that are important to an unbelieving husband, and perhaps to his career, just because you are a Christian.

2. Be more relaxed and less condemning. Roll with the punches instead of making too much out of too little too often.

3. Work as hard at improving yourself and becoming the woman your husband wants you to be as you want him to work at improving himself and becoming the man you want him to be.

4. If you married in direct disobedience, admit your sin, confess it, then get on with your life. Christ died for that sin on the cross and piling guilt on yourself will only make you more critical

of your husband's unbelief. You'll want him to come to the Lord to undo your mistake.

5. Have a Christian confidant—someone you can trust—to dump on when the going gets rough. Complain to and pray with her rather than nagging your husband or announcing his faults to your entire Bible study in the form of a prayer request. (That's disrespectful!)

6. Maintain a close relationship with the Lord. Study, read the Bible, pray, and obey. Concentrate on Christ; He's the only One who is perfect, anyway.

The apostle Paul noted that, "The woman is the glory of man" (1 Cor. 11:7). Solomon said, "He who finds a [true] wife finds a good thing, and obtains favor of the Lord" (Prov. 18:22 Amplified). A First-Peter-Three wife is a *true* wife: a favor from the Lord to her unsaved husband, a "good thing" who brings him pleasure and happiness. Ultimately, she can provide that necessary "God-element" that may change his life for eternity.

Workshop

1. Look up each passage of Scripture about submission. Write who is to be submissive and summarize in your own words how they are to do this.

	Who	How
a. Romans 13:1		
b. Ephesians 5:21		
c. Colossians 3:20		
d. Titus 3:1		

	Who	How
e. Hebrews 13:17		
f. James 4:7		
g. 1 Peter 2:13-15		
h. 1 Peter 2:18		
i. 1 Peter 5:5		

2. First Peter 3:2 states that the unequally yoked wife is to be respectful to her husband. Each of the words listed below is a synonym for respectful or respect, but each has a slightly different meaning. Look up each word in the dictionary and write its definition in the blank.

a. Polite _____

_____

b. Attentive _____

_____

c. Obliging _____

_____

d. Accommodating _____

_____

e. Admire _____

_____

f. Value _____

_____

g. Appreciate _____

_____

h. Venerate _____

_____

i. Honor _____

_____

j. Esteem _____

_____

3. In this chapter we discussed how your attitude, or the things you say about your husband, can affect peoples' thinking and cause them to form preconceived opinions about him. Based on statements you have made recently, and the attitudes you convey, write a character sketch depicting what you have shown or told others about him. Be honest!

_____

_____

_____

_____

_____

_____

_____

_____

_____

_____

_____

Portrait of a Marriage

Now that we have seen what a wife should be, let's take a realistic look at God's perspective on marriage and what an unequally yoked wife can expect from it.

Does it have to be a hotbed of conflict and controversy, or is it possible to have a happy, balanced relationship even if her husband is an unbeliever?

I asked a large group of women whose husbands are not saved in what ways they would expect their marriages to be different if their husbands came to the Lord. The obvious, and most predominant answer, was that each would have the assurance that her spouse would go to heaven when he dies. They also felt there would be better communication because their husbands would possess the Holy Spirit and the ability to understand the things of God.

But beyond those two basic spiritual considerations, their list of expectations reads like that of many women who are married to Christian men. They envisioned that once their husbands were saved they would get their priorities straight, be more sensitive and considerate, spend more time with their wives, be more open with them, have the same standards for raising children, and have matching desires about lifestyles.

And while such changes may gradually evolve when a husband comes to Christ, in many ways Christian husbands fail to live up to their wives' expectations in these areas, too. Salvation and perfection are not synonymous. I once heard a pastor say that if you take a person with a bad temper and a nasty disposition and get him saved, you'll have a Christian with a bad temper and a nasty disposition because the transition to sainthood takes time.

Rather than wishing things were different, all of us have to admit that, for the most part, our marriages only will be as good or as bad as we make them. And any unequally yoked wife can have a "Christian" marriage, to the extent that she is willing to implement God's standards into her performance and the relationship itself.

Immediately after Peter recorded the guidelines for unequally yoked wives, and some instructions to husbands, the Spirit directed him to pen a verbal portrait of an ideal marriage. Let's apply those standards specifically to an unequally yoked situation and explore what a Christian woman who is married to an unbeliever can do to be blessed in her relationship.

STAYING IN TUNE

God's formula for a fruitful marriage contains five "lets," the first of which is, "Let all be harmonious" (1 Peter 3:8). The unequally yoked wife must do everything within her power to keep her marriage in tune. The forces of evil will be working overtime to create disharmony and friction. The world will invade her territory and try to disrupt her family. But instead of letting Satan disturb her marriage, she must be a peacemaker and do whatever she can to eliminate discord; to balance the cacophony of her husband's unbelief with the new song God has put in her heart.

A balanced perspective is the key to maintaining harmony. Sheila shared that she was causing a lot of disharmony by overreacting to everything her husband did. "Whenever he'd light a cigar, I'd huff and puff more than he did. I'd correct him, like I do the children, if he said a swear word. And I acted as if his playing softball on the company team was an unforgivable sin. I was always losing my cool and that created all kinds of tension."

The Lord spoke to Sheila one day in Bible class when she read Proverbs 25:28: "Like a city that is broken into and without walls is a [woman] who has no control over [her] spirit."

"That hit me right in the heart and I realized that was my problem. I wasn't controlling my spirit and was turning into a nasty old nag who was making life miserable for her family."

Once Sheila realized she actually was causing dissension and hostility by rebelling against her husband's unbelief, she was able to control her responses and create a more tranquil atmosphere in their home. She is able to manifest the fruit of the Spirit and her unsaved husband is not, so she should draw on God's resources to bring harmony to the relationship.

SYMPATHY BEGINS AT HOME

The next "let" for an ideal marriage is, "Let all be . . . sympathetic" (1 Peter 3:8). Wives are to hurt for and with their husbands. Since they are one flesh, it seems reasonable that when a husband is in pain or suffering emotional conflict or depression, his wife cannot help but be affected by it. She should identify with his hurt, just as Christ identifies with ours.

Hebrews 4:15 says, "For we do not have a high priest who cannot sympathize with our weaknesses, but one who has been tempted in all things as we are, yet without sin." This ministry of sympathy offers a unique opportunity for an unequally yoked wife to stand in Christ's place, as a sympathetic priest in her husband's life, until such time as he relinquishes his life to the Lord.

The Christian wife must sympathize with her unsaved husband's weaknesses, just as Christ sympathizes with hers. She should hurt for him, remembering what it was like to be an unregenerate sinner. And she can bring him into the presence of God, through prayer: "Draw near with confidence to the throne of grace," petitioning the Lord on behalf of her husband. When she does, she will "receive mercy and [will] find grace to help in time of need" (Heb. 4:16).

It would be easy for her to harden her heart against the manifestations of her husband's unbelief, but she dare not because Christ does not. He sympathizes, and she must, too. She cannot be judgmental or self-righteous, because she is still a sinner although she has been saved by the grace of God. So when she feels resentment and frustration building up in her because of her husband's ungodliness, she must remind herself that "Christ died for the ungodly" (Rom. 5:6) and that "God demonstrates His own love toward us, in that while we were yet sinners, Christ died for us" (Rom. 5:8). Being sympathetic will create a bond in the union as nothing else can.

BE HIS BEST FRIEND

A third "let" is, "Let all be . . . brotherly" (1 Peter 3:8). This is a reference to the friendship aspect of the marriage. A wife isn't only to be a housekeeper and sexual partner to her husband. She is also to be his best friend. Friends do things together. They laugh, have fun, and enjoy one another's company. They are there to help when little emergencies arise or when no one else is around.

Frequently, unequally yoked wives nurture bitterness and jealousy in their husbands by neglecting this partner facet in their marriages, while cultivating deep friendships with believers. The wife is responsive to her Christian friends. She raves about the pastor, respects the rulers at her church, and holds God's Word in high esteem, but treats her husband like a second-class citizen. It becomes obvious to him that she prefers spending time with people from the church. She is loving and responsive to the needs of her brothers and sisters in Christ but neglects the man she married.

Difficult as it may seem, every rule of conduct which God says applies to us as Christians, also applies to an unequally yoked wife in her marriage. An old adage notes that "charity begins at home." If the unsaved husband is to be won without a word by his wife's godly behavior, and she slights him to spend time with Christians, she is failing through example.

HANDLE HIM WITH CARE

The fourth "let" is, "Let all be . . . kindhearted" (1 Peter 3:8). Marriage partners are to be soft-hearted toward each other; compassionate, gentle, tender, merciful. Interestingly enough, those are all attributes of God. Many times in the Gospels Christ looked at the masses of lost souls who were following Him, asking for hope, clinging to His garments, hanging on His words, and He had compassion on them. He was moved in His soul with care and concern. He identified with their infirmities, joys, and needs.

I once heard a pastor define mercy, or kindheartedness, as not giving someone what he deserves. An unsaved husband may deserve his Christian wife's anger, impatience, and criticism, but, because God has commanded her to be benevolent, she must not retaliate. Instead of being aloof and critical, she should be warm and understanding: merciful.

Christ taught that those who are merciful "shall receive mercy" (Matt. 5:7). He stressed going the extra mile, even if it is against your will, rather than giving up. "Whoever shall *force* you to go one mile, go with him two" (Matt. 5:41).

Jesus spoke against seeking revenge and instructed us about just how far we should go with his kindheartedness concept. "You have heard it was said, 'An eye for an eye, and a tooth for a tooth.' But I say to you, do not resist him who is evil; but whoever slaps you on your right cheek, turn to him the other, also" (Matt. 5:38-39).

God's mercy is so limitless that He is reluctant to give the most vile, unsaved sinner what he deserves. He holds back His wrath and judgment against the unbelieving husband because He so desperately wants him to repent and be born into His kingdom. "The Lord is not slow about His promise, as some count slowness, but is patient toward you, not wishing for any to perish but for all to come to repentance" (2 Peter 3:9).

If God, who would be perfectly justified in retaliating, restrains Himself because He is merciful, an unequally yoked wife must have that same mind-set: thanking the Lord for each day He mercifully spares her husband from final judgment, because He wants him to be born into eternal life.

PUT HIM FIRST

The last "let" is, "Let all be . . . humble in spirit" (1 Peter 3:8). In an ideal marriage, the partners are self-sacrificing, not self-promoting. Paul defined a humble spirit this way: "Do nothing from selfishness or empty conceit, but with humility of mind let each of you regard one another as more important than himself; do not merely look out for your own personal interests, but also for the interests of others" (Phil. 2:3-4).

The unequally yoked wife who has a humble spirit will lay aside her privileges in Christ in order to minister to her unbelieving mate. She will be motivated by love, not selfishness. She will want her husband to be saved for his benefit, not for her personal convenience. She will never think that she is better than her husband, or more worthy of God's love and grace. She will remember that *his* spiritual needs are more important than hers, because she has the Lord and he does not.

And, she will look out for his interests, protecting his reputation, doing what she can to build his self-esteem, respecting his right to believe as he chooses. His rights will take precedence over hers if she has "this attitude in [her] which was also in Christ Jesus" (Phil. 2:5).

The more I study and read the Bible, the more blessed and amazed I am at how deeply God understands our human frailties. He knows we tend to fight for our territory and become defensive and belligerent when we are threatened, so He tells us to be harmonious. He knows we dwell on our own hurts more than on those of others, so He asks us to be sympathetic. He knows we are not naturally friendly to anyone who causes us discomfort or inconvenience, so He commands us to be brotherly toward our husbands, who often, according to our opinion, impose themselves on us.

He knows we like to get back at others and give them what we think they have coming to them, so He says we must be kind-hearted. And He knows our enormous propensity for pride, so He requires that we possess a humble spirit. None of those qualities are natural or normal for us, so He educates us about our lacks by telling us what we should be.

GETTING EVEN

We see how thoroughly He knows our human nature by what He commands us *not* to do. "Be harmonious, sympathetic, brotherly, kindhearted, and humble in spirit; *not* returning evil for evil or insult for insult" (1 Peter 3:8-9). Those are two important principles for a successful marriage. One deals with actions, the other with words.

Returning evil for evil is the childish attitude of "he did this to me so I'll do this to him." Nothing could be more destructive in a relationship, especially in a marriage where one person is a Christian and the other is not. Chances are that in the unequally yoked situation, the believing wife may have more "evil" dumped on her so she could, in essence, have more things to strike back about.

We are warned against doing this. Proverbs 20:22 says, "Do not say, 'I will repay evil'; Wait for the Lord, and He will save you." And in Proverbs 24:29 we read, "Do not say, 'Thus I shall do to him as he has done to me.'" Retribution has no place in the life of any Christian.

Annette tried to get even. She told me how angry she was when her husband, Jim, joined a bowling league from work. They didn't bowl until nine at night, but instead of coming home for dinner, the team all went out to eat before they bowled. They also practiced for three or four hours every Saturday afternoon, and the women's team from the office went to both the practice and dinner with the men's group.

There is no doubt that this was an imposition on Annette. She was stuck with their two preschool children when Jim was gone and had no one to relieve her on the evening he bowled. She didn't like it that he was with those other women in a social situation twice a week. So she decided two could play at that game and she enrolled in a night course at the local junior college.

She left the house as soon as Jim got home from work and usually went out for coffee afterwards with some people from class. She and the children also started going to lunch on Sundays after church with a group from her Sunday school class.

"It got so Jim and I never saw each other. And we were both angry and snappy. We never had a decent conversation. I was miserable. Paying him back wasn't any fun at all. I decided I didn't want to live like that."

One night, when she was supposed to go to class, she took the kids to a friend's house, got dressed up, prepared a candlelight dinner, and hung a big "I'm sorry" sign over the door. Jim was elated when he walked in. They talked the whole thing through and ended up getting a baby sitter on his bowling night so Annette could go to dinner with the group, then watch her husband bowl. She dropped her night class but has decided to take some daytime courses once the children start to school. She learned that repaying evil for evil is hurtful and self-defeating.

Whereas not returning evil for evil deals with our deeds, returning insult for insult deals with what we say. When someone verbally assaults us, we want to counterattack. We want to get in our fair share of the comments, to have the last word, to win the argument. Because this is our natural response, God stresses that this kind of behavior cannot exist in a marriage.

Many unequally yoked wives told me that when they start trading insults with their husbands they automatically start quoting Scripture and throwing the Lord at them, which is exactly what they have been commanded not to do. As Crystal put in, "Railing on each other isn't exactly godly behavior. I may win an argument but I won't win Karl to Christ."

Rather than returning insult for insult, or shooting verbal barbs at each other, Scripture teaches that we are to give a blessing instead of an insult. (See 1 Peter 3:9.) Regardless of what her husband says, the unequally yoked wife should not counter in kind, but should say something to build him up or enlighten him, and to make him happy.

Since it is so hard to control the tongue, frequently it is better not to say anything rather than replying at all. I am not suggesting the "silent treatment" or pulling the old, "I'm not speaking to you" routine, but simply not saying anything until tempers settle and minds are not consumed with defensive thoughts. Someone once said, "It often shows a fine command of the language to say nothing."

The problem with trying to talk things through when someone is being verbally abusive is that it is normal to defend ourselves against what is said. The more that is said, the more danger there is of saying the wrong thing. The more words we utter, the harder it is to control the quality of the content, so it may be best to say nothing. The Proverbs stress the value of silence in heated situations: "An angry man stirs up strife, and a hot-tempered man abounds in transgression. He who restrains his words has knowledge, and he who has a cool spirit is a man of understanding. Even a fool, when he keeps silent, is considered wise; when he closes his lips, he is counted prudent" (Prov. 29:22; 17:27-28).

If we verbally retaliate, we end up speaking harshly. We choose phrases that will hurt the person we love the most. We use our words as weapons. We make cutting remarks. "There is one who speaks rashly like the thrusts of a sword" (Prov. 12:18). We lash out and wound to get even. We are hurt, so we want to hurt back, but instead we end up losing control and hurting ourselves.

I am not advising that the unequally yoked wife let her husband verbally abuse her, that she never talk with him about her feelings, or never disagree with him. I am saying I believe Scripture teaches that the time to deal with heated issues is when they have cooled off; when a problem or disagreement can be approached sensibly and calmly; when the need to avenge has diminished and emotions are not out of control.

Communication should take place when the circumstances are

right for it; when both parties can listen with their hearts and their heads, and when they have had an opportunity to think about what needs to be discussed. "Like apples of gold in settings of silver is a word spoken in *right circumstances.* The heart of the righteous ponders how to answer" (Prov. 25:11; 15:28).

Don't *not* communicate, but do use common sense about how and when.

THE ONE FLESH RELATIONSHIP— GOD'S STANDARD FOR ALL MARRIAGE

Satan loves to see husbands and wives miscommunicate, and since sexual intercourse is the most intimate form of marital communication, he will do anything he can to get an unequally yoked wife to use her faith against her husband. There is no place where the devil is more active than in the area of sexual relationships.

Some unequally yoked wives told me that once they came to the Lord their sexual desire for their unbelieving husbands decreased. Many said they feel or have felt guilty about their various sexual activities or about enjoying them.

Jerri was distressed when we talked. She confessed that until she had become a Christian she and Rex had had what she described as a "free-wheeling, passionate" sexual relationship. "We liked to try new things and have sex often. But once I accepted Christ, it's like something snapped inside of me. I don't think we should be doing things like we did before. I want our marriage to be pure and I guess somewhere, down deep, I think that since I became a Christian, sex is dirty."

Her reaction and concern are not unusual, but they are unnecessary and groundless. We have already seen that God means for a wife to be a sexual partner for her husband. The actual act of sexual intercourse consummates a marriage. It is the only act in the marriage that belongs exclusively to the husband and wife; that shuts out all other family members.

It is that mystical union that defies mathematics, taking two separate individuals and melding them into one entity. Just as the Christian becomes one in Christ and merges totally into Him at the moment of salvation, a husband and wife become one when they engage in sexual intercourse and merge totally into each other. This is not only a physical happening. Body, soul, and spirit permanently interfuse. Two become a single unit that cannot be divided.

There is no separation. Christ said a husband and wife have been joined together by God and that no human force should be allowed to penetrate their oneness. They have been cemented and molded to each other. And this one flesh relationship is God's standard for marriage—all marriage—regardless of the spiritual standing of either party.

Because this is the most intimate portion of any marriage relationship, God has demanded that it not be invaded by any other person. Adultery is forbidden. Because Satan knows how important this particular form of oneness is, he tries to intrude upon it; to demean and degrade it and create guilt about it.

THE IMPORTANCE OF YOUR BEDROOM MINISTRY

In 1 Corinthians, chapter 7, the apostle Paul gives instructions about sexual behavior to the church in Corinth; a church, incidentally, that was overrun with men and women who were unequally yoked. So he speaks not only to Christians who are married to Christians, but to believers who are married to unbelievers. The first thing he does is establish that sexual relations are a required part of marriage. He warns that if a husband or wife doesn't fulfill his or her obligations in this area, he or she may cause the partner to commit sexual sin by seeking satisfaction elsewhere.

"But because of immoralities, let each man have his own wife, and let each woman have her own husband. Let the husband fulfill his duty to his wife, and likewise also the wife to her husband" (1 Cor. 7:2-3). Unequally yoked wives, take note. There is no mention about the spiritual status of either the husband or the wife. That is immaterial to the point the Holy Spirit is making. If a wife does not fulfill her sexual duty to her husband she may drive him elsewhere, especially if he is not restrained by any commands from the Lord.

This doesn't mean it is "wrong" not to want sex at times. A woman's sexual appetite will vary. And there are times when everyone wants to be left alone. But saying no on occasion is not the same as withholding.

Smart wives, loving wives, compassionate wives don't ration their husbands; they don't set rules for frequency or prescribe the time, place, circumstances, or manner.

Dr. Herbert J. Miles, in his book *Sexual Happiness in Marriage,* states, "You are a prudent wife when you look on sex as an opportunity to bless your husband."[1] This is especially meaningful in the case of an unequally yoked relationship.

But, just because the sexual relationship is intrinsic to every marriage, does that mean "anything" goes? Was Jerri's desire for purity valid? Paul answers that, too. "The wife does not have authority over her own body, but the husband does; and likewise, also the husband does not have authority over his own body, but the wife does" (1 Cor. 7:4). So a wife should be willing to fulfill her husband's sexual needs in ways that are pleasing and stimulating to him.

Hebrews 13:4 states that the marriage bed is undefiled—that it is already pure and holy because it is part of a God-ordained, God-blessed institution. I believe this means that anything that is not physically harmful and is mutually acceptable to both parties is permissible.

The vividly descriptive passages in Song of Solomon also attest to this. And in Proverbs, while Solomon repeatedly condemns extramarital sex, he extols the virtues and pleasures of sex within the boundaries of marriage. "Rejoice in the wife of your youth. As a loving hind and graceful doe, let her breasts satisfy you at all times; be exhilarated always with her love" (Prov. 5:18-19).

Genesis 3:16 states that God has given a wife a sexual desire

---

[1]Herbert J. Miles, *Sexual Happiness in Marriage* (Grand Rapids: Zondervan Publishing House, 1976).

for her husband. If it is not there, or is not as strong or constant as it should be, she should pray and ask the Lord to awaken it. She may have a physical problem so a check-up and counsel from her doctor is advisable. Her marriage may be so deficient in other areas that she cannot respond sexually.

Or, subconsciously she may be withholding herself because her husband is an unbeliever.

Barbara told me that she went through a stage, after her conversion, when she felt as if she was dirtying herself if she let her husband touch her. But as she prayed and sought counsel, she realized she was withholding to punish Phil for not accepting Christ, too.

Her present perspective, in her own words, is, "I am a Christian so I'm indwelt by the Holy Spirit. When we have intercourse, Phil gets closer to God than at any other time, because he is closer to me. So I always pray for the Lord to make His presence felt when we make love."

Basically, what each unequally yoked wife needs to do so she can be at ease in her sexual relationship is develop a biblical perspective about sex and separate God's criteria from the ways of the world. Most important, she must believe that God wants and expects her to minister to her husband in the bedroom.

Now let's look at some of the sexual problems unequally yoked wives face. These problems, incidentally, are not exclusive with Christian women who are married to unbelievers. They are universal in nature, but may cause more concern for a woman who has to decide alone what her moral and spiritual sexual standards should be.

WHEN HE DOESN'T COMMUNICATE

Since sexual intercourse is the most intimate form of communication in a marriage, lack of communication in other areas may affect a wife's performance in the bedroom. Overall, sex is more comprehensive to a woman than it is to a man. His physical responses are more responsive to outside stimulation and he isn't as readily turned off by the harsh words of an hour before, nor is he as affected by his environment, such as children in the next room or having the lights on.

Many unequally yoked wives are sexually cool because their husbands will not openly communicate with them, but expect them to respond in bed. Ideally, sexual intercourse should be one form of marital communication, but not the only, or even the most important one. Sexual rapport doesn't just happen. It is created.

A woman can have her sexual attitude affected by the total life's setting, much more than a man. For a man, sex is primarily physical, whereas for a woman it is an all-inclusive act that encompasses much more than what happens in the bedroom. Generally, men are aroused by externals while women are aroused by internals.

What a husband communicates to his wife over the dinner table and how supportive he is of her as a person, his willingness to be open and loving through his words and deeds, are as important to her as what he does in bed.

But, even if an unbelieving husband is uncommunicative and perhaps insensitive, especially toward spiritual things which matter so much to his wife, she can still build a good sexual relationship by using it as the starting point for communication, rather than the culmination of it. She can use the intimate closeness of intercourse to open the door to other forms of communication.

There are several ways she can do this. She can ask for his opinions and counsel, rather than complaining that he doesn't notice when she needs his help. She can ask him questions about his job, his associates, his life, letting him know she cares and is concerned about him. She can talk to her husband about her feelings as they are preparing to have relations. As he approaches her with his sexual needs, she can, as she responds to him, open herself to him emotionally and let him know that she needs for him to share his thoughts with her as much as he needs her to share her body with him.

She should be appreciative and thank him in some way when

he listens and talks with her (despite the results). She should tell him how much it means to her when he is willing to be available. Women need to remember that it is usually more difficult for a man to show and verbalize his true feelings, to get down to a personal intimate level in conversation, than it is for a woman. This isn't because he doesn't feel as deeply, but because in our culture we have conditioned men not to be outwardly responsive. Therefore, a mellow sexual setting, where there is no danger of rejection, may open the door for him to explore other ways of expressing his thoughts and feelings.

Above all, a wife must never withhold sex because her husband doesn't communicate in other areas. This will only compound the problem. She can use their sexual relationship to cultivate the kind of trust, warmth, and closeness that build toward better communication in all areas.

WHAT'S OVER IS OVER

Another common sexual problem many unequally yoked wives face is that of failing to bury the past. With emotions so tied to sex, how can she forget the problems and impurities and worldly infractions her unbelieving husband has introduced into their marriage? The answer is, she can't. In her book *Key to a Loving Heart*, Karen Burton Mains profoundly notes, "We as humans are simply incapable of dealing with sin, either our own or that of others against us."[2] That's why we need a Savior. We cannot handle sin!

So, the unequally yoked wife must be willing to let God deal with her husband's sin, because she can't. She has to relinquish grudges, stop nursing old wounds and petty hates. The Bible teaches that we *must* forgive others. "Whenever you stand praying, forgive, if you have anything against anyone; so that your Father also who is in heaven may forgive you your transgressions" (Mark 11:25).

---

[2]Karen Burton Mains, *Key to a Loving Heart* (Elgin: David C. Cook, 1979).

It may seem as if God is asking us to do the impossible. Actually, He is reinforcing the idea that unforgiveness is a sin and that we must be willing to let God forgive others, just as He has forgiven us. The Lord "has not dealt with us according to our sins, nor rewarded us according to our iniquities" (Ps. 103:10), yet too often that is what we do in human relationships.

If an unequally yoked wife chooses to deal with her husband according to his sin, she will try to punish him, and part of her retaliation will take place in the marriage bed.

The only way she can forget the injustices and problems of the past is to ask God to forgive her unforgiveness, to heal her emotions, and to let God forgive through her. She has to let go, relinquish the past. As she does, her sexual relationship with her husband will improve.

TRY TAKING THE INITIATIVE

Men, like women, want to know they are needed. A husband may know that his wife needs him to earn a living, repair leaky faucets, take the kids to the ball game, and mow the lawn, but he also wants to know that his wife desires him sexually, just as much as he desires her. So it is both normal and preferable, at times, for the wife to be the sexual aggressor. It is her way of telling her husband that she needs him.

In the case of an unequally yoked relationship, many husbands are keenly aware of the spiritual barrier that exists, so if a Christian wife is willing to institute sex, it is a statement to her man that she wants him regardless of that difference. It is proof to him that she does not intend to let God come between them.

One of the greatest blessings a husband receives is when his wife takes the initiative. Those are the times he cherishes in his heart, just as a woman cherishes an unexpected gift or bouquet of flowers. A couple's sex life will be very one-sided and vital lines of communication blocked if the husband always has to be the one to institute sex.

No wife should be afraid to experience a variety of approaches with her husband. She should feel comfortable in her undefiled marriage bed, which has been sanctified by the Lord, to experiment and learn. Her eventual aim in her sexual relationship should be total freedom for both her and her husband, the kind of freedom Adam and Eve experienced when they "were both naked and were not ashamed" (Gen. 2:25).

THE BOTTOM LINE—BLESSING

What will happen, even in an unequally yoked marriage, if a wife adopts God's standards for an ideal marriage? She will be happy. Peter says she was called into her marriage relationship for "the very purpose that [she] might inherit a blessing" (1 Peter 3:9). What an exciting promise! She inherits a blessing from God. *He* takes notice of and regards her efforts. The joy and satisfaction she sustains in her marriage do not depend entirely on her unbelieving husband but on her Lord.

First and foremost, the unequally yoked wife must remember that she is the bride of Christ and that her heavenly Bridegroom loves her with an infinite love. He "loved [her] and gave Himself up for her, that He might sanctify her" (Eph. 5:25-26), so He can capacitate her to be a serene, sympathetic, merciful, humble wife to her earthly husband. He can help her build her marriage into a positive reflection of His grace and love.

Workshop

1. Look up each of these passages about peace and write a sentence telling how you can use the verse to build harmony in your marriage.
   a. Romans 12:18 _____

   _____

   b. Romans 14:19 _____

   _____

   c. Galatians 5:22 _____

   _____

   d. Colossians 3:15 _____

   _____

   e. 1 Thessalonians 5:13 _____

   _____

2. Look up each passage of Scripture about repaying evil for evil and write a sentence explaining what action it suggests you take when someone sins against you.
   a. Leviticus 19:18 _____

   _____

   b. Matthew 7:1-2 _____

   _____

c. Luke 6:37 _____

_____

d. Romans 12:17 _____

_____

e. Colossians 3:13 _____

_____

f. 1 Thessalonians 5:15 _____

_____

3. Look up each "proverb" about proper speech patterns and
   write a sentence telling how it could help a marriage relationship.
   a. Proverbs 15:1 _____

_____

   b. Proverbs 15:23 _____

_____

   c. Matthew 12:34 _____

_____

   d. Colossians 4:6 _____

_____

   e. James 1:26 _____

_____

   f. James 4:11 _____

_____

Hurts, Heartaches, and Hindrances

As we have seen, God has set forth many practical scriptural guidelines for marriage. Following them will greatly enhance the relationship, but it will not eliminate problems. It's one thing to study a beautiful blueprint and quite another to build a happy marriage.

No marriage is perfect. Hurts of all kinds do occur, especially in unequally yoked marriages. Christian women who are married to unbelievers face heartaches and hindrances in their marriages that Christian women who are married to Christian men normally don't.

Yet, a large majority of them eventually adjust to and overcome their difficulties. They are able to develop fulfilling marital relationships. They do this by admitting their problems and facing the reality of their situations. They have chosen to hold their heads high and let their human spirits be energized by the Holy Spirit. They are overcomers.

I asked the women I interviewed to share the greatest difficulties they encounter and practical ways they handle them. Each one, in some way, encouraged me to tell the readers of this book that happiness is possible in an unequally yoked situation, even if the marriage was in direct disobedience to God's command not to be unequally yoked. They stressed His grace and mercy and that it is possible to "do all things through Christ which strengtheneth me" (Phil. 4:13 KJV).

BUT I'M MARRIED TO AN UNBELIEVER!

The first thing they had to learn was how to overcome their guilt about being married to an unbeliever. Flo noted, "I realized that God disciplines us for all ongoing sin that should be forsaken. My marriage is not a sin, even though I married Tim when I was a Christian and he was not. I am not supposed to forsake it just because he isn't a believer. I love my husband and want to stay with him. That is not a sin. That's God's desire for my life."

Most women who married in deliberate disobedience are aware of, but do not resent, the Lord's discipline. Basically, they reap what they sow. Wanda has a marvelous perspective. "God allows the consequences of direct disobedience or ignorance," she says, "when knowledge was possible, to develop a strong faith and godly character in the Christian wife. Perhaps that is the only way He can infiltrate our selfish nature and win an unbelieving husband."

Some women are convinced that the unrelenting burden they feel for their husbands is a form of discipline. Joyce said she hurts continually because, "Don doesn't have the same desire for Christ as I have and he has no religious convictions. Seeing him stumble through life without the Lord is hard."

Sara's grief is that, "More than anything I want Brent to *feel* loved by God. He can't, and that breaks my heart." Barbara voiced the sentiments of all unequally yoked wives when she observed, "My marriage is not bad or difficult, but it lacks the God-factor all Christians so badly need."

Polly, a Christian widow who married a man thinking he was also saved and found out later he was not, believes that for several years she punished herself when she discovered Martin wasn't a Christian. "As we all do, I married with good intentions. I didn't want to be alone. I wanted my young daughters to have a father. Then when I realized Martin wasn't a Christian, I was totally devastated. I think I punished myself. My problems and struggles were of my own making because I was appropriating God's discipline, which I felt I deserved, instead of His grace."

Jan, who became a Christian after she married George, said she had never felt guilty because, "I was not spiritually accountable at the time. I didn't know God's will so I couldn't go against it. And, I've been forgiven. Christ nailed my sins to the Cross."

Regardless of how an unequal yoking occurred, a Christian wife must remember that, "there is therefore now no condemnation for those who are in Christ Jesus" (Rom. 8:1). She doesn't need to do penance for a sin that Christ erased on Calvary.

WHAT IF HE GOES TO HELL?

Almost all unequally yoked wives agree that the greatest heartache, and perhaps discipline, any one of them faces is the agony of knowing that when her unsaved husband dies he will pass into a Christless eternity and she will never see him again. Molly said, "It worries me so much because I know what hell is like and what Phil would go through if he dies without the Lord. None of us want to see our loved ones suffer, especially in the eternal pit of hell. That reality is a nightmare for me."

The only way for a Christian wife to cope with it is to put it into perspective in the light of the Word. She has to realize that rejecting Christ is her husband's choice. It isn't hers, because she has been told not to verbally witness to him. It isn't the Lord's, because it is His will that all come to repentance. God does not condemn anyone to eternal damnation. "God did not send the Son into the world to judge the world; but that the world should be saved through Him" (John 3:17). Rather, He provides the only way out—Jesus Christ.

Cecelia told me that the day she accepted the fact that her husband's salvation was dependent on him, and that God would never send him to hell because of anything she'd done, or to punish her for marrying him, she felt as if a huge weight had been lifted from her soul. "I have to leave him in God's hands and be the wife I'm supposed to be. I can't play the Holy Spirit, and I know Jack will have abundant opportunity to repent because God is just. God doesn't want him to go to hell, either."

On the other hand, the unequally yoked wife cannot live her life just waiting for her husband to receive Christ. She has to accept the fact that he could die unsaved. "I hope and believe," Cindy said, "but intellectually I know that everyone doesn't come to the Lord. That's a truth I have to face."

Neither should the Christian wife dwell on her husband's unbelief. If she thinks about it too much or too often, it will warp their entire marriage relationship.

"Sometimes when Mike and I have a real spiritual conflict, I get consumed by the fact that he isn't saved. It's almost as if he has horns, wears a red suit, and blows smoke. I see him as wicked and wayward," Karen admitted. "If I don't control it, it gets to the point where I think about it every time we have any sort of disagreement or he displeases me in any way."

Some unequally yoked wives admitted they want their husbands to become Christians as much for their own convenience as for their husbands' welfare. "I just get so tired of living with his worldliness and his carnal attitudes that I feel like crying out to the Lord to save me from him by saving him," Shirley confessed.

She suggested any time a wife starts concentrating on her husband's spiritual inadequacies that she pray out loud, and spiel her frustrations to the Lord until she has them off her chest. "God would rather I yell at Him about my anger and pain than yell at Paul."

CAN HE BE A GOOD FATHER?

Probably the most intense, overt problem the Christian wife faces in her unequally yoked marriage is conflict over raising the children. They see the difference in lifestyles between their parents and may decide to follow the ways of the world rather than the way of the Lord. The believing wife has to find some way to counter this and to expose her husband's sin to their children without putting him down or undermining his position as their father. Children learn so much by observing that it puts a heavy load on the Christian mother to set a constant example of godly behavior, and at the same time not be overly critical of her husband.

Also, "There is an inclination to use the children to evangelize your husband," Karla mused. "I can't get away with asking him to pray with me when we go to bed or cuddling up in his lap and asking him to read me a Bible story at bedtime, but Danny and Danielle can, and sometimes I put them up to it. That's not right. It should be spontaneous on their part."

The unequally yoked wife has to be as willing to let God handle the salvation of her children, as she is to let Him handle it with her husband. She does have an advantage as a mother, however, because she can play an active part in their spiritual upbringing, whereas her role as a wife, in the spiritual sense, must be passive. But many times the unbelieving husband fears that his wife is instilling her faith in the children to turn them against him. So she must be sensitive about when and how she trains them, and she must do it not in a way that demeans their father, but in a way that edifies and glorifies the Lord.

FEELING ALONE AND ISOLATED

Another major hindrance in an unequal marriage is that the believing wife has no human spiritual head in her home. While it is true that God can and will use her husband to direct her—this is accomplished through God's sovereign control of cir-cumstances and His literally superseding her mate's sin—in a Christian marriage it is done internally, through the indwelling presence of the Holy Spirit. So, although the Lord uses an unbe-lieving husband in practical ways, there is still a lack of spiritual communication between husband and wife.

Terri disclosed that "The thing that disappoints me most about my marriage is that I can't share anything spiritual with the person I love most. O sure, I tell him how God answers prayer and share what the Lord is doing, but he just doesn't understand. He believes in coincidence, not in answered prayer. I long for the day when he will be able to rejoice with me over the great things God is doing in our lives."

Spiritually, the unequally yoked wife is more or less on her own. Of course, she has the Holy Spirit, but in the reality of everyday living she has to decide herself if something is right or wrong in the eyes of the Lord. She doesn't have a husband to help her interpret her theology. She can listen to sermons, go to Bible studies, and develop Christian principles for living. But her husband may harass her for living according to God's standards, whereas a Christian husband will supplement a godly lifestyle.

Beth described it this way. "I'm very lucky because Andy supports me as a person and in what I want to do. He respects my beliefs, but there are times when I desperately need spiritual undergirding from him and he cannot give it to me. Sometimes moral support isn't enough."

No matter how many friends an unequally yoked wife has in her church, or how well received she is by the congregation, she still suffers from spiritual isolation. She has to go to church alone. Even if her husband does attend with her intermittently, she knows he is not there as an act of worship, or to fellowship with the Lord, but as a courtesy to her.

Compensation seems to be the solution to this dilemma. The unequally yoked wife must rely on the Lord for her spiritual guidance, rather than on her husband. She has to realistically face the fact that it is an impossibility for her husband to understand her spiritual needs, because he is not spiritually apprised.

Women in that situation advise that it helps to have a woman friend as a spiritual substitute for her husband. This should be someone who will be a prayer partner, who will sit with her in church, who will interpret the Scriptures with her, and who will give advice on spiritual matters. Sometimes the "friend" can be a Christian couple, so the unequally yoked wife will get input from a male perspective. But she must never build a separate friendship with a man. Unbelieving husbands don't understand about brothers in Christ, and an unequally yoked wife is emotionally vulnerable to Christian men.

These women who have "been there" further advise that an unequally yoked wife should concentrate on doing husband/wife things with her husband, apart from church, rather than resenting the fact that she can't be involved in church-related couples' activities. Adele verified the value of such an approach. "Recently a lot of families from our church went to a Christian camp for the weekend. I wanted us to go so badly that I got in a sulky mood and Irv never knew why.

"One afternoon, when I was crying and praying, telling the Lord how much I wished our family could go, He said, why don't you have your own family camp? I got so excited I could hardly stand it!"

By the time Irv got home, Adele had planned a family outing. He was elated at the idea. So they took the kids and camped on the beach for two nights and had a great time together. "I felt so close to the Lord, listening to the surf, meditating on His Word as I lay on the sand in the sun. And Irv mentioned several times how touched he was that I had suggested doing it. We had a wonderful family camp!"

Compensation. God can meet our needs wherever we are, in any circumstances.

DO YOU EXPECT TOO LITTLE?

As we have seen, there are many ways a husband's unbelief can affect the overall tenor of the marriage. One is that in the general context of the relationship, a wife may not expect as much joy, pleasure, or satisfaction from her marriage as she would if her husband was a believer. Many admitted they believed their marriages could never be as fulfilling as Christian ones are. "His unbelief takes the edge off our pleasure and the good things that happen because underlying it all is the fact that he doesn't belong to the Lord," Laura explained.

Such an attitude can be disastrous because it's a fact of life that most people live up to what we expect from them. So if a wife expects her husband to be responsive and loving, and to develop his capabilities and reach his potential, she will affect his performance positively. Conversely, if she sees him as inadequate and lacking something she possesses, and if she expects him to be remote or critical, chances are he will oblige.

Yvonne commented that when she first came to Christ, she was shocked at how her respect for Randy diminished. "It wasn't long until I realized I was suffering from a case of spiritual superiority. *I* had God and *he* didn't. And I had been acting as if I was better than him. That made him feel hurt and rejected. He stopped being the kind of husband he'd been before my conversion. He stayed away from me, didn't talk to me or kiss me as much. I didn't see it then, but I was driving him away.

"Finally," Yvonne continued, "one night when we were in bed I took him in my arms and told him I knew I had been a brat; that I had been acting like a snob and that the truth of the matter was that I loved him even more since I'd accepted Christ."

She asked me to caution all unequally yoked wives about lowering their expectations to accommodate their husbands' unbelief. "Many unsaved husbands love their wives, are good providers, tender lovers, competent fathers, and generally nice guys. They deserve to be accepted on their own merits, not because of their spirituality."

SOME ONE HAS COME BETWEEN US

Because the Christian's relationship with Christ is so precious and personal, it is easy for an unbelieving husband to become jealous of the Lord. Since this seems to be a widespread reaction, the unequally yoked wife must be extremely careful not to do anything that will make her husband feel he is in competition with God for her affections. Perhaps that is another reason why she is instructed to win him without a word. Verbalizing her intense feelings about God would only threaten her husband.

"Listen," Bob explained, "no man likes to feel he's second to anyone with his wife, and that includes second to God. Paula sure wouldn't like it if I spent as much time thinking about another woman as she does about Jesus."

Because the unsaved husband does not understand *who* Christ is, he cannot understand his wife's commitment to Him, and he may deeply resent the time she devotes to the Lord. Women who have faced this problem offered several suggestions to help alleviate it.

First, the wife must admit that her husband is probably jealous of the Lord, even if he doesn't know it. Second, she should not neglect her husband's needs, in any way, even for church or involvement in her personal ministry. Third, she must never make her husband feel she is choosing the Lord over him. She should not cut down on the quality or amount of time she spends with him to be involved in Christian activities.

Fourth, she must remember that it is Christ, and not the church, who demands her allegiance. She shouldn't confuse time spent with God with time spent at the church. Fifth, she should do Christian things—such as reading and studying the Bible, fellowshiping with other Christians, and instructing her children in the ways of the Lord—when her husband isn't around.

Lloyd, who is now a Christian, shared how it had aggravated him when Laura would sit and read her Bible in the evenings instead of watching television or playing Scrabble with him as she had before she became a Christian. "I didn't mind that she had found God or that she wanted to read the Bible, but I resented it that Jesus was intruding on my relationship with my wife."

Frequently, when a husband tries to share these kinds of feelings with his wife, she is less than understanding. Instead of being sensitive to his reactions and fears, she may think he is harassing her because of her faith, or being unreasonable by demanding equal attention. Many unsaved husbands are pleased that their wives have found something that makes them happier. They don't care if their wives go to church or teach the children about their faith, but they do care when God gets preferential treatment.

Who can blame them? The unequally yoked wife must be extremely careful not to let God become a barrier between her and her husband, even if it means neglecting some external religious rituals.

IF ONLY . . .

Another problem, which was mentioned in an earlier chapter, is that many unequally yoked wives idealize Christian marriages and dream about what their marriages would be like "if only he was a Christian." This causes friction and may make a wife resent her husband because he isn't a believer. Bea confessed, "When I fantasize about what our marriage would be like if Larry was a Christian, I feel I have to forgive him for not being one, but that's God's job and not mine."

In some ways, our churches compound this difficulty. Some unequally yoked women are embarrassed by the fact that their husbands aren't Christians. "I try not to tell anyone because when I do they always act like, oh, you poor thing. Or, they assume I deserve anything that happens because I was disobedient, which I wasn't, and married against the Lord's command about being unequally yoked. Then I get mad at Tony because he's put me in such a position by rejecting Christ."

Very few unequally yoked wives believe they are treated negatively by the Christian community, but they feel left out because so many church events center around husbands and wives. Melinda noted that, "I'm always made aware of *Christian* marriage relationships, in classes, in sermons, in the books I read and the lives I see, and it points up my own lack."

These women need to understand that if Christian marriages were so glowingly wonderful, there wouldn't be so many lessons taught, sermons preached, or books written on how to have a happy one. Christianity is not a panacea for all of our problems; it is a faith relationship with a God who is able to help us overcome sin.

HOW CAN WE AGREE?

God also can control an unbelieving husband during the decision-making process. God can affect what he thinks and does. An unequally yoked wife must not push or manipulate to get her way because she thinks it is God's way. If she does, rather than being a sounding board for her husband, she will become his conscience and block vital lines of communication. She will become his judge and jury. Instead of being available to listen to his problems and his ideas, she will pressure him, any number of ways, to get him to do what *she* thinks God wants done.

That is what Sarai did to Abram. God had appeared to him and promised that he would have multitudes of descendants, even though at the time he was almost ninety years old and they had no children. Sarai knew what the Lord had promised, but she got very impatient. Her human sensibilities wouldn't accept that she could become a mother, since she was far past childbearing age. She talked Abram into committing adultery with her handmaid, Hagar, so she would have a child for them.

Instead of waiting on the Lord, she blamed Him for her barrenness. "Sarai said to Abram, 'Now behold, the Lord has prevented me from bearing children. Please go in to my maid; perhaps I shall obtain children through her.' And Abram listened to the voice of Sarai" (Gen. 16:2).

Abram listened to the voice of Sarai! Never doubt the influence a wife has over her husband. She can use it either for God's glory or for her own personal gratification.

Well, Hagar conceived and Sarai was so jealous that she couldn't stand the sight of her maid. Sarai blamed Abram for what had happened. ("May the LORD judge between you and me"—Gen. 16:5.) So, in keeping with his wife's further wishes, Abram sent Hagar and her child into the wilderness. They would have died there if God had not supernaturally intervened.

Abram listened to his wife, and even today we are paying for the sinful counsel she gave him, because the Lord founded the Arab nations through Abram's and Hagar's son, Ishmael. "He will be a wild donkey of a man, his hand will be against everyone, and everyone's hand will be against him; and he will live to the east of all his brothers" (Gen. 16:12).

That conflict with the Arab countries still exists. It never would have happened if Sarai had not wrongly influenced her husband.

Although the unequally yoked wife is to be a helpmeet and counselor to her husband, she must influence him primarily through her prayers and her behavior. And, she must not assume that because she is a Christian, she automatically has a grasp on God's will.

The wife's role, then, is not to pressure her husband into doing things her way, but to trust God to lead him, through circumstances and external direction from the Holy Spirit. Jennifer has learned the secret of making such Spirit-controlled decisions. "Even if Gary isn't a believer," she observed, "I am. I have the Holy Spirit, so I can rely on the Lord to give us both the right answer, or to show me when to stand my ground or to back down, and to give me peace about giving in to my husband."

Here are some recommendations from unequally yoked wives who have mastered this technique. They warned that when God's will is presented to a woman through her unbelieving spouse, she may reject it unless she has let the Lord sensitize her heart to receive His message, regardless of who the messenger is. So first she should pray and ask the Lord to reveal His will to her.

Next, she needs to present her case based on facts, not on some ethereal spiritual reason. She should verbally communicate her reasons for feeling and thinking as she does. "The Lord told me" is insufficient proof for an unbelieving husband.

Also, she should state any objections she has to her husband's opposing view, but she must not attack him. She does not have to surrender what she believes is right, but she has to be willing to compromise, to reason with her husband, and to brainstorm for alternatives. Remember, that is God's suggested method in the decision-making process. "Come now, and let us reason together, says the LORD" (Isa. 1:18).

Attitude is important. She must abide by whatever rules of Christian conduct apply to the situation. She can disagree, but she musn't be disagreeable. She can reason with her husband, but not be unreasonable.

Finally, if a mutual decision cannot be reached and her husband isn't willing to wait or talk further, she will have to let him make the final choice. Then she must abide by it graciously. Sandy told me how, when Ken needed a new car, she really pushed him to get a station wagon. "The kids are getting older and I had visions of piling swarms of whooping big teen-age boys into my two-door sedan. But Ken was adamant. He wanted a sporty car, although he conceded to getting one with a back seat so he could carry four passengers."

"I was furious," she continued. "Until the fuel crunch. He gets great mileage and next year I'm going to get a compact wagon that also gets good mileage. If we'd have bought a big wagon, we'd be stuck with an unsaleable gas guzzler." She sees now that Ken's decision was best for their family finances. Even though his motives for wanting a smaller car may have been selfish, God bypassed those to accomplish His will in the matter.

WHO'S IN CHARGE?

According to my "experts," there are several danger zones where Christian wives tend to overstep the boundaries of their marriage roles, in the name of Christianity.

"We seem to think that because we have the Lord, we have to impose Him on our families," Kristen revealed. "We think we have the best answer, the godly solution, and that our husbands don't. So, we subconsciously try to run things 'God's' way, by manipulating."

There are four major areas where an unequally yoked wife must be careful not to inadvertently impose "God's" will on her husband. We have already discussed one; that of *making decisions*. She has to avoid the temptation to always have the final say, certain she knows what is best because she is a Christian.

The second area is *initiative*, where the wife, in order to control her husband's friends and social activities, becomes the instigator of all family plans. In many marriages, by nature, it seems the woman is the one who plans the dinner parties, evenings out, and backyard barbeques. But an unequally yoked wife may exclude her husband and bypass his wishes in order to create a more Christian atmosphere. She should include her husband when making plans and never accept or decline invitations without first consulting him. That is common courtesy.

Instead of shutting out her husband, she should make a special effort to minister to his friends. She needs to spread her Christianity around, not by hitting them over the head with her Bible, but by extending hospitality and withholding judgment.

The third area where role reversal sometimes occurs is *discipline*. Once a Christian woman starts using biblical standards for raising children, she may devalue her unsaved husband's input. She needs to learn how to incorporate godly principles into her and her husband's ongoing philosophy of parenting, which in many cases was established long before she came to Christ.

Marlene told how, before she accepted the Lord, when she and Harlan would be having a drink, sometimes they would give a sip to the kids. "As I grew in the Lord, I saw that wasn't right, so decided we shouldn't do it any more. I didn't tell Harlan how I felt, but the next time he did it, I hit the ceiling. I yelled at him that he was leading them astray and that he was breaking the law by giving liquor to minors."

Naturally, her husband was completely dumbfounded. She shared that after she had cooled off, she thought it through and apologized to him. "I told him the truth; that before I knew the Lord those kinds of things didn't matter, but now they do and that I feel as a Christian mother I have to protect my children from the dangers of alcohol. I told him I felt that by giving them a sip of beer we were telling them it's okay to drink and that when they are teen-agers they'll remember that."

She was blessed when Harlan not only understood, but said that was something neither of them had thought of before and it was a good point.

The unequally yoked wife must not try to be both a Christian mother and father to her children, but rather the best mother she can be. She should ask her husband how he thinks they should handle behavior problems and share new insights she gains from her study of the Word. They should plan together, as a couple, their strategy for disciplining the children.

Children are quite perceptive, especially when it comes to knowing what is going on between their parents. They will recognize, perhaps before their parents do, that there is an underlying friction. They will play one parent against the other, to get their own way. Consulting on minor matters eliminates that kind of manipulation and makes it easier to communicate about major ones. When an unequally yoked wife includes her husband in this way, she is showing him that she respects his opinion and position.

The fourth area where role reversal predominates is *finances;* where the Christian wife tries to "control" the money so she can give to the church or buy Christian tapes and books. Scripture does not state whether a husband or wife should handle the family finances, but it does clearly show that the man is to be the basic provider and that their life together is a partnership. So the issue here isn't who should keep the books, maintain the budget, or write the checks, but the fact that finances are a joint responsibility. If a wife tries to control the cash flow so she can give to the Lord, then she does not have a clear understanding of what He expects from her.

Jodi did just what we are talking about. Instead of asking John if she could give some money to the church each week, she started smuggling it out of her grocery fund. Whenever she cashed a check she would write it for a few dollars over, then put that in the offering.

You can imagine how startled she was when John unexpectedly asked her, "Don't they ever take an offering at your church?" She said her face flushed and she stammered an affirmative answer.

"Well," he asked, "don't you think if you are going to go there, you ought to contribute something?"

She was so ashamed that she broke down and confessed what she'd done. She told John that another woman she knew, whose husband didn't believe as she did, wouldn't let her give to the church. And in some instances, that's true. But that doesn't mean a wife should sneak money from the family budget. God knows why she is not contributing financially, if her husband won't let her give. He does not want her to resort to sinful methods so she can give. Often an open, honest request to work some kind of donation into their financial picture will bring a positive response.

Obviously, there are many ways an unequally yoked wife can minimize the hurts, heartaches, and hindrances in her marriage. She can concentrate on what God is doing in her and her husband's lives, instead of on the fact that he is not saved. She can respect his views about child-raising and treat him as an equal in parenting. She can keep her expectations within the realm of the possible when it comes to spiritual matters, but not lower them in an overall sense.

She can eliminate her husband's jealousy toward God by putting him first, in an earthly sense, and making their marriage a priority over even the church or Christian friends. She can refrain from idealizing Christian marriages and remember that most of the problems she faces are common to all marriages, and are not contingent on the fact that her husband is not a believer.

Finally, she can adapt her marriage standards and incorporate godly ones into an ongoing pattern that she and her husband believe are best for them, rather than trying to impose spiritual externals on him. As she does this, with God's help, the hurts, heartaches, and hindrances will subside.

Workshop

1. How many of these negatives are you able to overcome? Read each statement, then rate yourself by checking the appropriate column. Use pencil so you can erase as you re-check yourself periodically.

	Always	Usually	Some-times	Seldom	Never
a. I feel guilty about being married to an unbeliever.					
b. I concentrate on the fact of my husband's unbelief.					
c. I expect my husband to accept the spiritual things in my life.					
d. I have lower expectations for my husband and our marriage than I would have if he was a Christian.					

	Always	Usually	Some-times	Seldom	Never
e. I think my husband is jealous about my relationship with the Lord.					
f. Church attendance is an issue between us.					
g. God is a barrier between me and my husband.					
h. I dream about my husband becoming a Christian.					
i. I try to control my husband's choice of friends and social activities.					
j. To get my way, I unduly influence my husband.					

2. How well do you measure up in the light of the suggestions made in this chapter? Rate yourself.

	Never	Seldom	Some-times	Usually	Always
a. I am able to leave my husband's spiritual fate in God's hands.					
b. I think of my husband as a partner in parenting.					
c. My husband and I agree on the way our children should be raised.					
d. I have a close Christian friend in whom I can confide and who prays for and with me.					
e. I concentrate on doing husband/wife things with my husband.					

	Never	Seldom	Some-times	Usually	Always
f. I rely on God's directing me through my husband.					
g. I am a good sport when my husband disagrees with me.					
h. I respect his opinions, even when I disagree with him.					
i. I value him as a father to our children.					
j. I am open and honest about how I spend money.					

3. Write a private prayer to the Lord about the greatest heart-ache in your marriage. Tell Him exactly how you feel, what you feel, and why you feel it. Then commit it to Him for healing. (Write this prayer on a separate piece of paper and keep it private.)

Shouldering Spiritual Responsibility

As we've seen, in many ways the role of the unequally yoked wife and mother is identical to that of any Christian woman. She is to be a helpmeet, friend, sexual partner, and counselor to her husband. She is to train up her children in the ways of the Lord. But there is one way in which her duties are entirely different. She is totally responsible, in the human sense, for her and her children's spiritual growth.

A Christian husband is to some measure accountable for his wife's spiritual nurturing and development; he has been commanded to "love [her] just as Christ loved the church" (Eph. 5:25), and to do whatever he can to present her holy and blameless before the Lord. An unsaved husband is not concerned about his wife's spiritual maturity, nor is he involved in edifying her toward godliness.

Likewise, a Christian father is obligated, along with his wife, to "bring [up his children] in the discipline and instruction of the Lord" (Eph. 6:4), but an unbeliever is left to his own devices. So when a Christian woman is married to an unbeliever, she is responsible to fulfill those godly parental instructions and also to keep herself pure and holy. That is an awesome responsibility.

The fact that her husband is not saved means the unequally

yoked wife must carry out alone the Lord's spiritual desires for her children. In most instances, even though the father isn't a Christian, he has high standards about raising children. He wants them to be respectful, to be honest, to control their behavior, and to go to Sunday school and church. In some cases, this is not true. The father may be so caught in the world's system that he tries to ingrain sinful patterns into his children's lives, although he does not know they are harmful to the child.

Kim's husband thought he was doing what was best for his daughter by insisting she take birth control pills when she started dating, so she wouldn't get pregnant. Greg's dad felt it was wise to teach his son how to drink and smoke at home, so he wouldn't feel he had to run and hide to do it. Lori's husband believes everyone has to lie to survive, so he teaches their three children the value of manipulating the truth, to get what they want or to promote themselves. Those are only a few of the dilemmas unequally yoked mothers face.

WHOSE CHILDREN ARE THEY?

There are some basic things God requires of any parent, and these fall to the Christian mother in an unequally yoked marriage. She may not always be the one who carries them out, but she must be sure they get done. One is *discipline*—controlling the child and his circumstances, directing him by example, teaching him right from wrong, laying down standards for behavior, and punishing him when he disobeys.

Mothers and fathers are instructed, "Do not hold back discipline from the child" (Prov. 23:13). It is an essential part of their development. And this discipline, which forms their lifestyle and steers them toward adulthood, is to be carried out with a loving, godly attitude. Parents are warned: "Do not provoke your children to anger" (Eph. 6:4). "Do not exasperate your children, that they may not lose heart" (Col. 3:21).

So, not only must a Christian mother see that the right standards are taught and preventive measures taken, but she has to do it in a way that encourages her children and builds their sense of self-esteem. Screaming, yelling, and nagging will only defeat them, so even if her unbelieving husband indulges his moods, a Christian mother dare not.

Another parental responsibility that an unsaved husband cannot handle, but that the mother must, is *teaching her children the ways of the Lord.* He commands Christian parents, "You shall teach [God's commandments] diligently to your [children] and shall talk of them when you sit in your house and when you walk by the way and when you lie down and when you rise up" (Deut. 6:7). The believing mother must see that her children receive instruction from the Word and that God's precepts are ingrained into their thought and behavior patterns.

This is extremely difficult to do if her husband objects to overt spiritual instruction. Women whose mates are belligerent about this suggest that a Christian mother should pray with and read the Bible to her young children when her husband is not in the house. Bonnie observed, "I have Gwen and Glen alone with me for eight to ten hours a day. I can do a lot of teaching during that time. It's easier on all of us than making a production out of it when Pete's around." But, she must do it.

Also, she is to see that her children have Christian fellowship; that they attend church and in some way are ministered to and exposed to the corporate body of Christ. Most women said they simply insisted that their children be allowed to go to Sunday school, and few husbands objected. Others compromised and took them to week-night activities. The issue is not as much when they go as the fact that they do, and that they attend church often enough to develop an attendance pattern.

Also, church is the place where they will meet and make Christian friends, and should later be the base for their social activities. "I just know it's my duty before God to see that my children get formal religious training. I have to because my husband can't," Betty surmised.

Sue noted that as her children attend Sunday school and grow in the Lord, they better understand their father and why he acts as he does. "Even our four-year-old knows his daddy stays away from church and doesn't pray because he doesn't have Jesus in his heart. The more they develop spiritual insights, the less I have to explain to them. They feel more secure knowing their Sunday school class and teacher are praying for their daddy."

IS SUNDAY A BATTLEGROUND?

Not only is the unequally yoked wife responsible for the basic spiritual upbringing of her children, but she is also answerable for her own growth and maturity. This means she, too, must study the Word, pray, and follow God's admonition to not forsake assembling together with believers. (See Hebrews 10:25.) She can do many of these things when her husband isn't home, but what if he doesn't want her to go to church on Sunday?

Many unsaved husbands resent having their weekends interrupted. They feel the whole day is lost by the time their wives and children get home from church. "Lois acts as if lightning will strike her dead if she doesn't go to church on Sunday," Chris complained. "I'd like for us to go away for the weekend, or go to the desert or beach and spend the day, but to her Sunday is a sacred cow."

Lois is making problems for herself by drawing such a hard line. She is shutting out her husband and nurturing jealousy of the Lord in him. She is telling him, by her actions, that she would rather go to church and be with Christians than go somewhere with him.

There are several things an unequally yoked wife can do to keep church attendance from becoming a controversy. One, she needs to understand the difference between loyalty to the Lord and loyalty to the church. She is not forsaking the cause of Christ if she misses Sunday services. Some unsaved husbands are so unreasonable that they forbid their wives to go to church on Sunday. "Instead of causing a fight," Martha said, "I stay home with Ted, then go to weekday Bible study and listen to a tape of Sunday's sermon. I see to it that I read a Bible story to the kids every day and send them to church with friends, as often as I can. Then Ted and I have Sunday mornings to ourselves. That way the kids still get to Sunday school and my husband feels special, too." Christian fellowship and assembling together to pray and worship are important. When they happen is a variable. Rose said she was relieved when her pastor told her that the early church met every day and night, in homes all around the city. They ate, studied, and worshiped together whenever it was possible. Nowhere does the Bible say we have to go to church every Sunday morning. It says we are to meet together frequently, as a corporate group of believers.

A Christian woman who is married to an unbeliever may have to adjust her schedule to meet both his and her needs. She should not ignore, nor overemphasize, Sundays. Lil said, "I always went when I could, but I was always ready to make exceptions." Many women suggested that the wife ask her husband several days in advance if he wants to make plans for the weekend or if she can go to church on Sunday. That way he doesn't feel left out.

DIFFERENCES DON'T HAVE TO BE DEVASTATING

In the human sense, shouldering the total spiritual responsibility for herself and her children is an overwhelming task. It not only involves raising and disciplining the children in a godly manner, going to church, and studying the Word, but it also encompasses implementing God's behavior standards in everyday life situations. That, most unequally yoked wives agree, is where some fundamental difficulties arise. Conflicts over morals, spending money, social activities, and friends, are common.

"It gets lonely," Martha mused. "Lots of times I look like a party pooper. I'm the killjoy, the fall guy. Sometimes its just me and the Lord, but when it is, I remember His grace is sufficient."

How can an unequally yoked wife do what is expected of her, in a Christian sense, and still not invoke the wrath of her husband when she must, out of necessity, take a firm stand on scriptural issues? The overwhelming counsel of women who have learned from experience is that she should not make a "religious" issue out of the problem.

For example, if an unsaved husband wants his wife to do something dishonest, instead of saying such things are against what the Bible teaches, she should say they are against her personal moral principles. And it's true, they are. Karen was caught in that kind of quandary when her husband falsified their income tax. They file a joint return, so she had to sign it. He hadn't tried to hide what he was doing: padding their contributions list, including what she supposedly had donated to the church, and claiming personal expenditures as business deductions.

She knew she could not sign the return. "I wanted to yell at him and ask him if he didn't know that cheating on taxes is wrong, but instead I prayed a lot and asked my Bible study to pray, too. One dear, sweet grandma told me not to tell Will that God was the reason I couldn't sign. She suggested I write a list of all the reasons why I wouldn't, apart from the fact that it's against one of the Lord's commandments."

That's what Karen did. When Will asked her to sign it, she told him she couldn't because it went against her moral standards of right and wrong, and that, most of all, since falsifying income tax returns is a felony, he was asking her to be his accomplice in a crime.

"At first he was furious, accused me of overreacting, and used the old 'everybody does it' line. But I stood my ground, so he had no choice but to change the figures, because our tax was due and the forms had to be sent in with both of our signatures. It was hard not to give in to his pressure, but I didn't," Karen concluded.

Although she was resisting because she knew that signing the return would be breaking the law of the Lord, God never became an issue. But her husband saw that his wife is a woman who sticks to her deep, moral convictions.

TO GO OR NOT TO GO?

Social activities and friends are another source of conflict, but again, difficulties surrounding them can be minimized if an unequally yoked wife will use common sense. One problem she consistently faces is "to go or not to go." To what extent should a Christian wife expose herself to the world? Where should she draw the line? The general consensus of opinion, by women who have learned how to deal sensibly with such predicaments is, if it isn't a sin, go.

In other words, if an unbelieving husband wants his wife to go to an X-rated movie, that would be sin because she would be exposing herself to lustful, erotic, mental, and physical sexual stimulation. If he asks her to experiment with the possibility of an open marriage, that is sin, because Scripture clearly condemns extra-marital sex. If he asks her to lie for him, that is sin, because we have been commanded not to bear false witness.

But, if he wants her to go to an office party, where everyone will be drinking and using foul language, that is not sin. Connie said, "Look, I have the Holy Spirit within me and my body is His temple, so I just take my altar and go with Brock."

Many unequally yoked wives attested that by going with their husbands and participating in whatever way they could, they felt they strengthened their marriages. An unsaved husband can't help but notice the contrast between his wife, who is friendly, laughing, and having a good time, and those people who are loud and boisterous because they've had too much to drink. Her genuine enjoyment will overshadow their pseudo, artificially induced pleasure.

Some women believe that going to worldly social functions with their husbands creates opportunities to witness. Sally told how she met Beth, a co-worker of her husband's, at a dinner party at George's boss's house. "When I asked for a tonic water with a twist of lime instead of a cocktail, she asked me if I have a problem with liquor. I told her no, I just don't like to drink. We started talking and it ends up she has a secret drinking problem. Now I'm helping her with it, and we first met over cocktails."

Barbara stressed that no one can make her sin or detract from her godliness unless she lets him. She said that when she knows she is going into a worldly social situation, she fasts and prays that day, so God can fortify her to spiritually withstand the things that are offensive to her. "I ask Him to show me the lostness of the people there and give me opportunities, no matter how small, to share some of what I have in Christ with them."

HIS FRIENDS

Another problem centers around ongoing relationships. Many couples have similar interests, regardless of their spiritual status, and enjoy the company of the same kinds of people. Their individual friends are acceptable to both the husband and wife, and their mutual friends are ones with whom they have a lot in common. But sometimes, in an unequally yoked marriage, the believer's desires are so different from those of her unsaved mate that she cannot accept her husband's friends, or people with whom he wants them to socialize as a couple.

Frequently, an unequally yoked wife is afraid her husband's friends will lead him farther away from the ideals she is praying he will develop, or that if she accepts his choice of companions she will be condoning the relationships. Yet if she nags or overtly condemns his cohorts, she will only intensify the problem.

The women I interviewed suggested several helpful ways of approaching and dealing with this dilemma.

First, an unequally yoked wife must accept the fact that she is not responsible for what her husband does. She cannot force him to behave in a certain way, nor can she choose his friends for him.

Second, she should be aware that the more negatively she reacts to his choice of acquaintances and activities, the more he will resist her interference. He purposely may pick certain types of friends just to defy her wishes and to show her he is his own person.

Third, she should evaluate her husband's associates on the basis of their individual personalities and character, rather than on externals. Just because his buddies smoke, drink, or swear occasionally doesn't mean they are highly immoral. If they use drugs and engage in illegal activities, that's a different story. She has to learn not to overreact to normal worldly externals.

Fourth, she should use "reverse psychology," and instead of degrading or snubbing her husband's friends, she should help him cultivate deeper relationships with those who can offer positive input. Dana shared that she found that if she talked favorably about the friends she liked and felt were a good influence on her husband, and was hospitable to them, the less favorable affiliations eventually dwindled.

Fifth, the unequally yoked wife would be wise to see that her husband's friends feel comfortable and welcome in their home. "I used to cringe when I bought booze for Dave to offer his pals when they come over," Dana continued, "but I decided I'd rather have them hanging around our house, where I could have some influence on what happens, than sitting in some bar or going to a home where there is an 'anything goes' atmosphere."

Sixth, she must realize that just because her unsaved husband sometimes wants to go off alone with his friends, that doesn't mean he is deserting her or their family. "I used to resent it terribly when Brian would go fishing or hunting for a weekend, or when he'd go bowling or to a ball game with the boys," Kerri admitted. "One night when he asked if I'd care if he and five of his buddies went skiing the following weekend, I flipped. I ranted about how he was always looking for excuses to get away, which isn't true, and how selfish he was to want to spend our money on himself like that.

"After I calmed down, he very quietly asked me how I would feel if he'd have said those kinds of things to me when I asked him if I could go to the women's retreat our church had." Kerri confessed that she was so convicted she started to cry. "He'd been so sweet about my going. He kept the kids. I was so ashamed."

She says she learned that, in Brian's eyes, her going to a church retreat is no different from his going on a skiing trip and that her going to Wednesday night church is the same in his thinking as when he goes bowling. "It's something we do with our separate friends," she concluded.

An unequally yoked wife has to remember that all of her

husband's friends aren't wicked, lecherous people who want to lead him down the path of destruction, and that when they plan activities with him they aren't doing it to take him away from his home and family but because they enjoy being with him.

PRAY ALONE AND STAY TOGETHER

Ultimately, the only way a Christian wife can cope with the constant barrage of conflicts she faces is through prayer. Prayer helps her maintain her perspective and equilibrium. It is her source of godly wisdom, the microscope through which she can examine her actions and motives, and get direction.

We often quote the promise in James 1:5: "But if any of you lacks wisdom, let him ask of God, who gives to all men generously and without reproach, and it will be given to him." But, just as often we fail to apply it in the setting in which it was written. In context, James is saying we should ask for God's wisdom when we encounter various trials and when our faith is being tested; when we need the strength to keep on keeping on: "Consider it all joy . . . when you encounter various trials, knowing that the testing of your faith produces endurance" (James 1:2-3).

So it is during those times of conflict and tribulation, when the unequally yoked wife feels she is going to cave in, or that God has given her more than she can handle, or when she is forced to make decisions about the controversial areas we have discussed, that she can call on the Lord and know He will give her more wisdom than she needs. "My problem is that I usually do what I think is best without consulting Him first," Marcia reflected, "and then I end up in trouble."

Prayer also prepares a Christian wife for her husband's unreasonable or worldly reactions. It keeps her from giving up and quitting. "There are times when I'd like to just walk out and never look back," Alice said. "Then when I pray, God calms me and assures me that all wives feel that way sometimes. There's no other way I can keep things in perspective."

"I receive God's counsel by praying," Evy noted. "If I went to a Christian friend, a church leader, or my Bible study teacher every time Cliff and I have what seems like an unsolvable problem, I'd be running to someone all the time. If I keep asking people for advice, I can easily put my husband down or reveal private things that should be kept between the two of us. So I've learned to go to the Lord for help."

Many wives with unsaved husbands said that prayer equips them to accept, yet not be consumed by, the fact that the man they married is doomed to hell. Carolyn divulged her method for dealing with that anxiety: "When I get upset, sometimes even frantic, about Darrell's salvation, I pray until Jesus absorbs all of my fears and pain. I literally dump my husband's unbelief on Him, and when I do, He bears the burden of it so I don't have to. I think that's what 1 Peter 5:7 means when it says to cast all our anxiety on Him because He cares for us."

These women, who rely heavily on prayer, stressed that sometimes their communications with the Lord are shouting matches. They scream out their anger. They cry in frustration. They openly admit their feelings to their Savior. And, they pray very specifically for their husbands. "The plain old 'God bless Sam' variety won't do," Norma joked.

They also emphasized the importance of their role as intercessor for their unbelieving husbands. "Jerry can't pray for himself. Even if he went through the motions, unless it was a sincere prayer for salvation, God wouldn't listen to it. But I'm His child, and He listens to me," Carol stated confidently. "I've got a direct line to heaven and Jerry knows it. Regardless of how much he balks about my 'religion,' he relies on the presence of God in my life and my prayers for him."

A majority of unequally yoked wives have the same experience. They said that although they did not pray aloud for their husbands, in their presence, that they let their husbands know they were praying for them. "I don't make a big deal out of it," Sue noted. "I just tell him I'll pray for this or that in his life. And he appreciates it, as long as he's sure I won't ask my friends or Bible study group to pray, too."

Most unsaved husbands think they'll seem weak or look like bad guys if their wives ask other Christians to pray for them. It embarrasses them and wounds their pride, so a Christian wife should respect her husband's wishes and keep his prayer needs to herself, except in dire circumstances. She will lose his confidence if she doesn't.

Bill is a Christian but wasn't saved until fourteen years after his wife's conversion. He stressed that, "Nothing affects an unbelieving husband quicker or makes him madder than for him to find out his wife has been sharing their personal lives in the form of prayer requests. It's like an attack on his manhood."

An unequally yoked wife also needs to know what to pray for her husband. Her normal inclination will be to ask God to change the externals that bother her, that offend her godliness, that cause turmoil. She needs to grasp that underlying all of those manifestations of the old sin nature is the fact that his soul has not been regenerated through the new birth. While she knows it intellectually, she needs to deal with it practically, through prayer. Her basic petition for her husband must focus on his need to accept Christ as his Savior.

Many years ago I was taught a prayer method, to use for people who are not saved. It is a beautiful approach to the throne of grace and has proven effective. It is simple yet profound. First, you must go before the Lord and, through confession and repentance, cleanse yourself from any sin, confident that, "If we confess our sins, He is faithful and righteous to forgive us our sins and to cleanse us from all unrighteousness" (1 John 1:9).

Next, you praise God for who He is, quoting Scripture or words from your favorite hymns. Don't rush into His presence, but spend several moments concentrating on His magnificence. Then picture in your mind the person you are praying for. Visualize him as he is at that moment: engulfed in the darkness of sin, doing whatever deeds of the flesh that are reflections of his unsaved state. Verbally describe that person to God, as he is now. State his condition; if he's depressed, sick, lonely, whatever. Ask the Lord to help you pray intelligently for that person's needs. If words won't come, rely on the Holy Spirit, who, "also helps our weakness, for we do not know how to pray as we should, but the Spirit Himself intercedes for us with groanings too deep for words, and He who searches the hearts knows what the mind of the Spirit is, because He intercedes for the saints according to the will of God" (Rom. 8:26-27).

Next, imagine Christ reaching out to that person. Concentrate on Jesus' light. Visualize it penetrating the darkness of sin, erasing it with His dazzling brilliance. In your thoughts, bring the person you are praying for toward God's light and love. Don't ask for specifics, but commit him to the Lord, saying, "Lord, I ask that You shed Your light and love upon _____ and woo and minister to him through Your Holy Spirit."

Think about God's love; how Christ died for that person, how He is willing to receive him unto Himself, no matter what the person has done. Ask the Lord to create an identical love for that person in your heart.

Next, hand that person over to Jesus and envision Him wrapping him in His arms, completely submerging him in His light and His love. Ask Him to perform a mighty work in that person's life, to change him into the person He wants him to be. Then mentally commit the person to that position from then on. Every time you pray for him, think of him as being inundated with the person of Christ, as what he can become in Him, rather than how he exists in his present, sinful state.

If a Christian wife uses this method to expose her unsaved husband to God, she will find she is able to focus on what the Lord can do, rather than on what her husband is not. And somehow, holding him before Almighty God may allow the Lord to strike a responsive chord in his heart.

Above all, she must rely on prayer as the undergirding resource to enable her to shoulder the spiritual responsibilities God has privileged her to carry.

She must remember that Jesus is her yoke-mate and that His "yoke is easy and [His] load is light" (Matt. 11:30). Together, they can do whatever needs to be done.

Workshop

1. Part of a Christian wife's spiritual responsibility is the upbringing of her children. Look up each verse and answer the
   question.
   a. *Deuteronomy 11:18-19.* When are we to instruct our chil-
      dren in the ways of the Lord?

   _____

   _____

   b. *Deuteronomy 32:45-46.* Who is to teach children the law
      of the Lord and see that they obey it?

   _____

   c. *Proverbs 3:12.* What should motivate a parent to discipline
      his child?

   _____

   _____

   d. *Proverbs 29:15.* What happens if a child is punished? If he
      is not?

   _____

   _____

   e. *2 Corinthians 12:14.* What parental obligation is men-
      tioned here? What does it mean?

   _____

   _____

f. List after each verse what the duty of a godly child is. (Remember, these are things Christian parents should teach their children to do.)

(1) *Exodus 20:12.* _____

_____

(2) *Leviticus 19:3.* _____

_____

(3) *Psalm 119:9.* _____

_____

(4) *Proverbs 1:8.* _____

_____

(5) *Colossians 3:20.* _____

_____

(6) *2 Timothy 2:22.* _____

_____

(7) *Titus 2:6.* _____

_____

2. Since prayer is the power that enables an unequally yoked wife to shoulder her spiritual responsibility, she will be more effective if she understands what prayer is and how to intercede for her husband. To see what the Bible says are the prerequisites for answered prayer, look up each passage and write the qualifying factor.

a. *Psalm 66:18.* _____

_____

b. *1 John 3:22.* _____

_____

c. James 4:3. _____

_____

d. 1 John 5:14-15. _____

_____

e. Mark 11:22-24. _____

_____

f. John 15:7. _____

_____

g. Luke 11:9. _____

_____

h. Ephesians 6:18. _____

_____

i. Mark 11:25. _____

_____

j. Philippians 4:6. _____

_____

3. Intercessory prayer can be defined as asking God to act on behalf of someone else. The apostle Paul established a pattern which believers can follow when they pray. Read Colossians 1:9-12.

   a. Colossians 1:2. For whom is Paul praying?

_____

_____

b. List nine things Paul asks for.

(1) _____

_____

(2) _____

_____

(3) _____

_____

(4) _____

_____

(5) _____

_____

(6) _____

_____

(7) _____

_____

(8) _____

_____

(9) _____

_____

c. *Colossians 1:12.* How does Paul close?

_____

_____

Drawing the Line

When the phone rings at two in the morning, you know it's bad news or someone has gotten the wrong number. George sleepily groped for the receiver and after saying hello, handed it to me. Kathy was frantic. I could barely understand her, she was crying so hard.

As I questioned her, I was able to decipher that her husband had come home drunk—not an infrequent occurrence—and that he was in a rage. He had torn up her Bible, pushed her into the wall two times, and was threatening to hit her. She had run into the baby's room, grabbed him, then locked herself and her son in the bathroom. Finally, when Steve passed out, she put Gabe back in his crib and called me. "What should I do? I'm so scared. I'm afraid he'll hurt us," she rambled incoherently.

I told her to get dressed, bundle up the baby, take whatever she would need for them and get out as fast as she could. Since Steve had the only set of keys to their car in his pocket, I suggested she call her sister to meet her at the corner, rather than having her come to the house.

"But how can I leave?" she cried. Doesn't the Bible say it's wrong for me to leave my husband? Don't I have to stay unless he kicks me out?"

Unfortunately, although Kathy's intentions were good, her theology and common sense weren't. While her situation is extreme, it is not uncommon. A large number of Christian women live with unsaved men who are emotionally and/or physically abusive. Their home situations are not unlike those of the poor, well-intended people who get trapped into cults and are so brainwashed that they are afraid, and even feel guilty, if they leave to save their lives or their sanity.

As we saw in chapter 5, there are many problems an unequally yoked wife can face and handle. Sadly, some are insurmountable. This chapter is directed toward women who live under intolerable conditions of oppression and bondage; whose husbands constantly inveigh against them or bodily imperil them.

HOW MUCH IS ENOUGH?

The questions each of these unequally yoked wives must answer is: How much is enough? Does God expect her to tolerate vicious belittlement and/or physical attacks? Is she being nonsubmissive if she refuses to put up with continual maltreatment from an abusive mate? Since she probably cannot stop nor control his cruelty and censures, does she, in God's eyes, have the freedom to remove herself from the situation?

None of these questions are easily answered, nor is there one simple solution for all women who are married to men who are emotionally or physically abusive. But, as always, God's Word contains guidelines which the unequally yoked wife, whose husband is a tyrant, can use to help her decide what the Lord's will is for her individual plight and help her determine how much is enough; where to draw the line.

GROUND RULES FROM SCRIPTURE

In 1 Corinthians, chapter 7, Paul gives multiple instructions to Christians about what their conduct should be within the marriage relationship. He covers some issues that did not exist before Christ's death, including the situation of a Christian married to an unbeliever. Prior to the cross, the Jews were God's chosen people. After Calvary, anyone who accepted Christ as Savior became a member of God's family. As a result, there was a lot of confusion in the early church, because the Jews no longer held their selective position unless they placed faith in the risen Messiah. Those who did could be classified as believers; those who did not were outside the family of God.

Suddenly, there were Hebrew Christians who were married to Jews who were not Christians. So the question arose: Since under Old Testament law, Jews weren't supposed to marry unbelievers, should the Hebrew Christians who were married to Jewish unbelievers leave them? Consequently, the apostle addresses that issue, teaching new doctrine which had not been presented by Christ, while reiterating some things Jesus had taught.

Paul starts by reaffirming a previous teaching: "That the wife should not leave her husband . . . and that the husband should not send his wife away" (1 Cor. 7:10-11). He lays the foundational principle that there is to be no separation once a couple is married. Christ taught the same thing, emphasizing that, "What therefore God has joined together, let no man separate" (Matt. 19:6).

God's ideal is that a husband and wife stay married until one of them dies. Paul instructed Christians, "A wife is bound as long as her husband lives; but if her husband is dead, she is free to be married to whom she wishes, only in the Lord" (1 Cor. 7:39). So marriage is supposed to be a forever affair. But if a Christian is widowed, she is permitted to remarry, as long as she marries another believer.

The two basic rules concerning marriages are: Christians are to marry Christians, and once two persons wed they are never to separate or end that relationship. Because marriage is a temporal covenant and not an eternal one (there is no marriage in heaven), if a union is severed by the death of a husband or wife, the widowed one may remarry.

Paul also explains that the same standards apply to a Christian who is married to an unbeliever, "A woman who has an unbelieving husband, and he consents to live with her, let her not send her husband away" (1 Cor. 7:13). So the general rule is that an unequally yoked wife cannot separate from or divorce her husband simply because he is not a believer, which is what some men and women in the Corinthian church were doing.

They even had a good reason for doing it. According to Jewish custom, a Hebrew who united with a Gentile was unclean in God's eyes. His sin could be transmitted to the Hebrew, making him or her impure and unholy. That is why the Lord so vehemently condemned mixed marriages. God's chosen were never to defile their separateness unto the Lord by co-mingling with heathens. And because the Corinthian Christians didn't fully know or understand the New Covenant, they thought any marriage that involved a believer and an unbeliever had to be terminated, or they would be unclean.

Paul assures them that under the New Covenant there is no communication of uncleanness such as there was in the Old Covenant. "The unbelieving husband is sanctified through his wife, and the unbelieving wife is sanctified through her believing husband; for otherwise your children are unclean, but now they are holy" (1 Cor. 7:14). Such a marriage union is lawful and, rather than the unbeliever tainting the believer, the Lord uses the Christian spouse to cleanse, or sanctify, the one who is not saved!

This does not mean an unbelieving husband will go to heaven because he is married to a Christian, but it does mean that he will receive some privileges and benefits because of his close contact with one of God's children. He will benefit from "spiritual fallout," as the Lord showers his wife with His blessings. Also, as we read in 1 Peter 3:1, constant exposure to godliness may lead him into an eternal relationship with the living God.

Paul doesn't stop his instruction after laying down the rules. The Holy Spirit led him to amplify his statements and teach the exception to the rule: "Yet if the unbelieving one leaves, let him leave; the brother or the sister is not under bondage in such cases, but God has called us to peace" (1 Cor. 7:15).

Rather than demanding that an unequally yoked wife stay in a situation where she is abused, defamed, and oppressed; where she is tortured by the temptations that such mistreatment put in her path, our precious Lord gives her an option. He does this because, "Just as a father has compassion on his children, so the Lord has compassion on those who fear Him. For He Himself knows our frame; He is mindful that we are but dust" (Ps. 103:13-14). He understands her humanity and takes pity on her.

LEAVING IS MORE THAN WALKING OUT THE DOOR

A Christian woman who is facing emotional or physical abuse needs to understand both the terminology and the implications in this verse, so she can act on it within the dictates of her own common sense and conscience. The word "leave," as it is used in 1 Corinthians 7:15, means to depart or let go. While this most obviously refers to a physical separation, the concept of letting go embodies more than mere physical absence.

Since thought always precedes action, I believe we can assume that abuse or cruelty are outward manifestations reflecting a mental state of abandonment of the essence of the marriage. So, although Paul is dealing with physical separation, certainly there can also be a psychological severing, an emotional letting go, that is just as devastating and real as a mate's actual departure.

Scripture does not deal specifically with this problem of abuse, but Christ's attitude and certain biblical statements can help us draw conclusions about how to respond to it. The Gospels are saturated with statements about and examples of Jesus' compassion. He was especially tender toward women and children. Think of how gently He approached the woman at the well; how respectful He was to the woman caught in adultery; how He met Mary's needs by teaching her as she sat at His feet; how, during excruciating agony on the cross, He committed His mother to the care of His friend, John.

In the fifth chapter of Ephesians, the apostle Paul commanded husbands to "love [their] wives, just as Christ also loved the church and gave Himself up for her" (Eph. 5:25) and to "love their own wives as their own bodies" (Eph. 5:28). Christ, in love, sacrificed His life for the church. This example is the antithesis of abuse. I have yet to hear of any man who verbally abuses or batters his wife claiming he does it because he loves her, or because it is how he wants to be treated himself.

It appears, then, that any man who constantly mistreats and maligns his wife, who wounds her psychologically and/or physically, has "let go" and departed from the intent of his marriage vows. He may be living under the same roof and sleeping in the same bed with her, but if he neglects her needs and destroys her as a person by attacking her body, soul, or spirit, *mentally he has left!* If he is cold, cruel, and uncaring, he has already separated himself from her, even if he shares a house with her. In his sick mind, the relationship is over.

The idea of leaving, then, can legitimately include the unbelieving husband mentally and/or emotionally abandoning his wife. The final act of "leaving" may mean he will physically remove himself, but the psychological process leading up to that moment may manifest itself in ongoing abusive conduct.

The Bible says that when this happens a Christian wife is to let him leave. The Lord does not expect or want her to suffer mental or bodily harm at the hands of a husband who is supposed to sacrifically love her. God does not want her to be oppressed or incapacitated by fear. Quite the contrary, "the sister is not under bondage in such cases" (1 Cor. 7:15), and any woman who is physically harmed or verbally belittled, insulted, or harassed by her husband is under bondage. Any wife whose husband controls her mind and activities with threats or brutality is enslaving her.

In this same chapter, Paul reminds us, "You were bought with a price; do not become slaves of men" (1 Cor. 7:23). God did not buy an unequally yoked wife out of the slave market of sin so she could be under bondage to another human being. He purchased her with the blood of Christ and freed her so she could voluntarily become *His* bondservant.

She has to draw the line if her husband consistently oppresses her, by whatever means. In Luke 14:26, Jesus said, "If anyone comes to Me, and does not hate [by comparison of her love for Me, her] own father and mother and [husband] and children and brothers and sisters, yes, even [her] own life, [she] cannot be my disciple." She has the right and responsibility to choose freedom in Christ over bondage to an abusive husband, if he makes it impossible for her to fulfill her Christian calling.

We have already seen that submission is voluntarily choosing to yield or surrender to someone. When God instructs wives to subject themselves to their husbands, He is asking them to surrender to their husbands' love and God-given position. Nowhere does Scripture imply that the Lord expects a wife to accede to verbal castigation or physical assault.

Many times women who are in this position convince themselves that they would be unsubmissive if they fled. So, instead of retreating and protecting themselves and their children (who may be scarred for life from exposure to continual abuse), they become passive; but passivity is not the same as submission. Whereas submission is voluntary, passivity is forced oppression. Whereas submission allows for individual dignity, passivity breeds self-hatred, and eventually a wife who subjects herself to abuse starts believing that she deserves it!

She convinces herself there is no way out and that she is only getting what she has coming to her. This is especially pronounced in cases where Christian women knowingly married unbelievers. Frequently they stay to punish themselves, to pay the penalty for their sin. Their attitude is: I got myself into this, now I'm stuck with it. So, they become passive. It is vitally important that a woman who suffers maltreatment in her marriage draw the distinction between submission and passivity.

Also, some women stay because of guilt. They believe that their faith in Christ is the reason for their husbands' abusiveness, so they think that staying is a cross they must bear—part of their suffering for Christ. They need to realize that there is an immense difference between being persecuted for the Lord and for righteousness' sake, and being physically or emotionally abused by a man who is a tyrant. Although an unbelieving husband might use his wife's faith as an excuse for attacking her, that is not the real reason. Men who batter or consistently demean their wives are emotionally ill. The unequally yoked wife who is being vilified by her husband does not have to submit to his tirades. God does not ask her to yield to outrageous attacks.

Sometimes a Christian woman who is being harmed by her mate stays because she believes that the Lord will protect her no matter what her husband does. Candy thought that, until Glen shot her. Eleanor thought that, until Ed fractured her back and skull when he threw her down the stairs. Emily thought that, until Howard burned down their house when he was spaced out on pot and booze and fell asleep on the sofa with a lighted cigarette in his hand. Their three-month-old daughter suffered severe burns over 30 percent of her body and was in the hospital for months.

Claudia thought that, until she had a mental breakdown. Her children had to be put in foster homes while she recovered because the court ruled that her husband was not a fit father.

If there are children involved, the repercussions of living under such disparaging conditions can leave them with lifelong scars. Scripture teaches the importance of example. We are warned not to associate with fools, liars, fornicators, idolators, blasphemers, or hot-tempered people, because if we do we will imitate their behavior. Statistics show that many parents who are child abusers and many men who batter their wives were themselves mistreated as children, or came from homes where one or both parents were abusive. Like begets like. Removing herself and her children from danger isn't selfish, isn't sinful, isn't unsubmissive—it's smart.

God hasn't called the unequally yoked wife to live in a spirit of fear and mental instability but of "power, and of love, and of a sound mind" (2 Tim. 1:7 KJV). He hasn't chosen her to live in a state of confusion, not knowing what to say or do next, or what tirades her well-intentioned responses might bring. "God is not a God of confusion but of peace" (1 Cor. 14:33) and "has called [her] to peace" (1 Cor. 7:15).

WHAT ABOUT DIVORCE?

A close examination of Scripture seems to indicate that God does not require a Christian woman to stay with an abusive husband. She will, however, have to determine for herself whether she should get away from him temporarily—perhaps a legal separation—or if her situation is so intense and hopeless that she can no longer live with him at all. The important thing is that, once he *leaves*—forsakes her psychologically and/or physically, or abandons or deserts their marriage union—she has those options.

Her concern should center on protecting herself and her children, if she has any, and not merely on ending the marriage. One decision will lead to subsequent decisions and actions: a separation, whether temporary or permanent, may raise the question of divorce; if a divorce occurs, there is the question of eventual remarriage. All these decisions have scriptural implications.

Since God's standard does not intend for a permanent separation to take place, I would recommend that she let her unbelieving husband initiate divorce proceedings, if it comes to that. If they separate, she might find it necessary to seek legal counsel, even if a divorce isn't pending. But she should not take the first steps toward permanently terminating the marriage.

If her unbelieving mate files for divorce, she should "let him leave." If God lets the marriage end, through the actions of her husband, then she should accept that. If not, she should remain as sensitive to the letter of the law as she possibly can, which means, as a Christian she should not file for divorce; not because the Lord wants her trapped in a debilitating relationship, but because she must do everything she can to remain guiltless. Also, she is staying open to the possibility of a reconciliation, should her prayers be answered in the affirmative and her unbelieving mate come to a knowledge of Christ, repent, and want to re-establish their relationship.

Could she ever make an exception and file for divorce herself? This is ultimately a personal decision based on specific circumstances. Many churches believe that a Christian can sue for divorce if her partner has committed adultery. They consider sexual infidelity to be "biblical grounds," based on Christ's statement in Matthew 19:9, that "whoever divorces his wife, except for immorality, and marries another commits adultery."

The question of grounds is significant, because Scripture implies that the privilege of remarriage depends on the spiritual validity of a person's divorce.

It is my personal opinion that there are no "biblical grounds" for divorce. I have several reasons for believing as I do. The first rests on the fact that since marriage was sovereignly instituted by the Father to be a lifetime, irrevocable, one-flesh relationship, it would be contradictory of Him to provide a way for us to violate it by providing grounds for dissolution.

The second reason is that there are other sins which, although they do not invade the intimacy of the marriage bed, are as ghastly, and sometimes more debilitating to the relationship than adultery. I know numerous couples who have salvaged their marriages after one or both have been physically unfaithful. Saying adultery is grounds for divorce makes it an "unforgivable" sin, in the human sense.

I have even had women tell me they wished their husbands would commit adultery so they could get a divorce and not be considered the guilty party by the Christian community. And if a wife is looking for an excuse, a reason to end the marriage, she may even subconsciously drive her husband into the arms of another woman, in order to establish grounds.

The third reason is that God hates divorce. (See Mal. 2:16.) He would not instruct one of His children to seek it. Christ made that very clear when He was being questioned by the Pharisees on this matter. "Is it lawful," they asked, "to divorce . . . for any cause at all?" (Matt. 19:3). Jesus reaffirmed God's ideal and intention by responding, "What therefore God has joined together, let no man separate" (Matt. 19:6).

They immediately countered Him with an example from Scripture. "They said to him, 'Why then did Moses command to give [a wife] a certificate and divorce her?" (Matt. 19:7). And in

His reply, the Lord Jesus Christ establishes what I believe is the only reason God, in His grace, allows divorce to exist at all. "He said to them, *'Because of your hardness of heart,* Moses *permitted* you to divorce your wives; but from the beginning it has not been this way*"* (Matt. 19:8). This passage implies that the adultery Christ referred to in Matthew 19:9 is a blatant reflection of a hard heart. Divorce would thus be permissible, though not required.

In his book, *Divorce and Remarriage in the Church,* Stanley Ellisen notes that the clarification by Jesus about adultery "should not be seen as allowing laxity in granting loopholes for divorce. It was rather intended to emphasize the devastating effect of extramarital sex."[1]

God does not command divorce, or require it, or even condone it. From the beginning, His desire has been that every marriage be a loving, monogamous, lifetime relationship. He did not design it with termination in mind, but He does *permit* it for one reason: hardness of heart. The Lord God is loving and merciful, so He tolerates man's vilification of marriage, just as He does other breeches of His perfection that are perpetrated by our sin. Divorce is never His will nor His ideal, but in some circumstances it is allowed.

Stanley Ellisen further notes that, "We should first of all recognize that [the Bible] does not present [divorce] as an option, but as a last resort, if not a last rite."[2] Steven Brown, pastor of Key Biscayne, Florida, Presbyterian Church, believes "that God has never affirmed divorce. This includes Christians and non-Christians. Marriage is part of the Adamic covenant and is therefore binding on everyone."[3]

He further observes that physical abuse is intolerable. "I fall

---

[1]Stanley Ellisen, *Divorce and Remarriage in the Church* (Grand Rapids: Zondervan, 1980), p. 53.

[2]Ibid., p. 48.

[3]Steven Brown, "Divorce and Remarriage: Ministers in the Middle," *Christianity Today* (June 6, 1980).

back on the argument concerning hardness of heart. A wife beater certainly does not have a 'soft' heart . . . and I don't think it's stretching the point to call such a man 'unfaithful' to his wife and their marriage covenant. There is nothing subjective about black and blue marks and broken bones."[4]

Hardness of heart, which results in ongoing mistreatment or physical danger to a wife or the children, is the point of no return. It is where an unequally yoked wife can draw the line. It comes packaged in many ways. Solomon depicts it as being unresponsive to God's desires, neglecting His counsel, and refusing His reproof. (See Prov. 1:24-25.) In the first chapter of Romans, Paul says a foolish, darkened heart manifests itself by not honoring God as God or giving thanks to Him; and in sexual immorality, idol worship, and a depraved mind.

Once a person sets his soul in cement and refuses God's touch, nothing can be done to save that person. Once a husband hardens his heart against his marriage, nothing can save the marriage. So God permits separation or divorce to rescue the one who is pliable and salvageable.

EXAMPLES FROM REAL LIFE

I want to tell you about three different women who have faced this kind of situation, and how each has handled hers. Debbi was only nineteen when she married Doug. Neither were Christians at the time. They had two babies in three years. It wasn't long before Debbi realized Doug was a spoiled child himself. He floated from job to job, never helped with the children, and literally kept her barefoot and pregnant. She accepted Christ as the result of the witness of a Christian neighbor.

Doug got into drugs, first smoking pot, then taking pills. He drank heavily and frequently became violent when he was drunk. He started hitting her and she was afraid he would do something to one of the children. "I just packed up and left," she drawled in her southern accent.

---

[4]Ibid.

"I didn't know then what the Bible said, but I just couldn't picture Jesus wanting me to get my teeth knocked loose or one of my babies going hungry because their daddy was spending his money on pills and booze."

Debbi was fortunate. She had friends who took her in. Doug disappeared shortly after that and it's been three years since she's heard from him. His family doesn't know where he is, either. She has filed a missing persons report and has been counseled by a Christian attorney to file for divorce. "He's probably dead," she ponders, "and I want a chance to live a normal life."

Kristie's situation is markedly different from Debbi's. Her husband, Hal, is an engineer. He's handsome, generous, and obviously loves his wife and children. Kristie is, as she put it, "crazy about him." They are compatible in many ways.

Their problem was that once Kristie accepted Christ, Hal became viciously abusive about anything that had to do with the Lord. He burned her Bible and once locked the children in a room and tied Kristie to the bed to keep them from going to church. He would scream and yell filthy things at her about God, Christianity, and the church.

"It was like he was a completely different person. Most of the time he was his usual, kind, sweet self. Then suddenly, for no apparent reason, he'd fly into a rage and attack me. Afterwards he'd refuse to discuss it and go on like nothing had happened."

Kristie was frightened. "He was so uncontrolled I was afraid he might kill me or hurt one of the kids. It was a nightmare. To see Hal acting that way was horrible."

She sought her priest's counsel. He felt that Hal's outbursts were demonic; that Satan was fighting for his soul because he knew he was going to lose it to the Lord. He encouraged her to take the children and leave without saying a word any time Hal started a tirade. He told her, "I don't care if you are in the middle of cooking dinner, taking a shower, or asleep at four in the morning. Just get away from him when this happens."

She did as he suggested, although it meant living a roller coaster existence for over a year and a half. Hal went to his

doctor and was tested for possible physical causes for his behavior, but there were none. He attended group therapy sessions,
but that didn't help. Finally, one evening when he and Kristie
were home alone, he flew into a rage when he found her Bible
open on a nightstand.

He threw her around the room and ripped pages out of the
Bible. "I couldn't get away from him so I just cried out to God, as
loud as I could. I said, 'Oh Lord, please help me. Help Hal. Save
me! Save him!'"

She had tears in her eyes when she told me that suddenly he
stopped, looked at the torn Bible in his hands and at his wife,
who was cowering in the corner, fell to his knees and said, "Oh
yes, God, save me!"

After he accepted Christ, the outbursts stopped and he was
able to share with Kristie some frightening religious experiences
he'd had as a child. Their family is now happily united in Christ.

Whereas Kristie didn't actually leave Hal, but removed herself
when he was being abusive, Mary separated from Curt. She knew
he was not a Christian when she married him, but she was
certain she could convert him in short order. She also knew he
was a party-goer and that he liked to drink, but she did not know
he was an alcoholic.

They had five children over a period of ten years, during which
time Mary was active in her church and raised her children in the
ways of the Lord. Curt's drinking got so bad he couldn't keep a
job and was in an alcoholic stupor a lot of the time. Mary had to
go to work to support the family, and when she did, he quit
working altogether. It didn't help that his parents pampered and
babied him, even gave him money, which he spent on liquor.

Finally, Mary had enough. She was convinced that Curt had
no intention of trying to straighten himself out or of being a
husband to her and a father to their children. So she asked him
to move out. Although he was in his thirties, he went home to
mama.

That was six years ago. He is still drinking and has never
contributed one cent to their support since he left. The children

maintain contact with him and see him irregularly, more out of obedience to the Lord's command to honor their father than out of desire, since he has not been a father to them.

Mary has never taken legal steps about separation or divorce. She says she is perfectly happy as she is and doesn't need to go any further. She doesn't believe that, as a Christian, she should file for divorce and since Curt hasn't, they are still married. She doesn't know why he hasn't, but thinks it might be because his only interest is alcohol. He just doesn't care enough one way or the other to do anything about the mess his life is in. Being married doesn't hamper him in any way.

Sadly, there are other Christian women who are caught in quandaries such as these. It should help them to know that God, in His mercy, has provided relief for them. They do not have to be destroyed by their husbands' sin but can live victoriously, free from needless oppression and bondage, secured by God's love and His promises. There is a way of escape.

Workshop

1. Look up each passage, then write what requirement is stated for a husband's behavior.

   a. *Proverbs 5:15-19.* _____

   _____

   b. *Ecclesiastes 9:9.* _____

   _____

   c. *1 Peter 3:7.* _____

   _____

   d. *Malachi 2:14-16.* _____

   _____

   e. *Ephesians 5:25.* _____

   _____

   f. *Ephesians 5:29.* _____

   _____

   g. *Colossians 3:19.* _____

   _____

   h. *1 Timothy 5:8.* _____

   _____

2. Look up each reference about the heart, then answer the question.

   a. *Deuteronomy 6:5.* What function of the heart is mentioned here?

   _____

   _____

   b. *2 Chronicles 12:14.* What causes sin?

   _____

   _____

   c. *Psalm 34:18.* What kind of heart desire pleases God?

   _____

   _____

   d. *Psalm 51:10.* How can a heart be cleansed?

   _____

   _____

   e. *Psalm 57:7.* What results when a person's heart is fixed on God?

   _____

   _____

   f. *Proverbs 4:23.* How can we protect our hearts from sin?

   _____

   _____

   g. *Matthew 5:8.* What benefit is there in having a pure heart?

   _____

   _____

    h. *Matthew 15:19-20.* What things did Jesus say overflow from a hard heart?

_____

_____

    i. *Ezekiel 11:20-21.* How Does God regard an obedient heart? A hard one?

_____

_____

    j. *Hebrews 4:12.* What part does God's Word play in purifying the heart?

_____

_____

    k. *Exodus 7:13, 22; 8:15; 9:12.* What results from a hard heart?

_____

_____

Do's for Marital Happiness

I would like to introduce you to three women who are unequally yoked. Each of them has been married to an unbeliever
for many years.

Shirley beams when she talks about her husband. She recently
told a group of women that she thinks she is the luckiest woman
alive to have married a wonderful man like Andrew. She ad-
mires, respects, and obviously loves him. They are happily
married.

Elaine and David have been married for thirty-five years. They
have had ups and downs, but haven't we all? She had some
difficulties raising the children, but she was such a good wife in
all respects that her husband gave her a free hand in the spiritual
realm. Now they are enjoying retirement—traveling together
and savoring the companionship. They have a good marriage,
one that many of David's unbelieving friends envy. They are
happily married.

Donna and Ray are both approaching fifty. Donna is the only
one in her family who knows the Lord; her husband and three
grown children are unbelievers. They are a close-knit family and
have fun together. She participates in her husband's hobby, auto
racing. Although she has had to miss church many Sundays to

134 / Beloved Unbeliever

travel around the state with him, she has done it willingly. He is openly proud of her. They are happily married.

What's the moral of these stories? *You can be happy though unequally yoked*, without compromising your faith or your dedication to Christ. In this chapter we will look at some do's that these, and other women like them, have put into practice that have made their marriages happy, enjoyable, and fulfilling. Some review what has already been discussed, some are new.

EXPECT TO BE HAPPY

We all anticipate that when we marry it will be a pleasurable, rewarding experience. No one enters into a lifetime relationship expecting to be unhappy. So what happens in an unequally yoked partnership that makes so many wives unhappy? Could it be that they expect to be miserable, to have insurmountable problems, because their husbands are unsaved? It is a fact that we get out of life what we put into it and expect from it.

No relationship in the world is flawless. The God-man relationship is hampered by human sin. The employer-employee association suffers from personality, ambition, or expectation conflicts. The parent-child bond is marred by generational or moral differences. And, *any* marriage embodies inherent flaws, but deficiencies do not mean the entire relationship is tainted or ruined.

Charlotte M. Yonge said, "Happiness? That would mean more contented with my station in life, striving to derive all possible benefits from it, to BEAUTIFY rather than alter it."[1] The unequally yoked wife has to believe she can be happy and fulfilled in her marriage. Rather than being discontented because she is married to a man who is not a Christian, she must concentrate on cultivating and enjoying peace and happiness where God has placed her. Instead of trying to alter her status, she should seek to beautify and derive every possible benefit from her life as it is. She should plan to be happy, and she most likely will be.

---

[1]Charlotte M. Yonge, "Goldust," *Something to Live By*, Dorothea S. Kapplin (Garden City: Doubleday, 1945).

EXPECT HIM TO BE UNREASONABLE

The fact that a Christian is married to an unbeliever does not have to cause unhappiness in the marriage. But it will, unless the unequally yoked wife expects her unbelieving husband to be unreasonable about spiritual things. Conversely, he probably thinks she is unreasonable about earthly matters.

To him, the Bible is no better guidebook for living than his favorite "how-to" or self-help book. He undoubtedly enjoys going to the movies more than he does going to church. Sin is not an issue to him, as it is to his wife. Her godliness is threatening, convicting, and confusing to him. He does not understand it.

I have found that we Christians have a tendency to impose our personal idea of spirituality on everyone else. Wives, in particular, think they have the right and ability to set the terms for what their husbands' spiritual responses should be. I remember what our pastor told me when George accepted Christ. He warned, "You must never forget that your husband's spiritual life is in the Lord's hands. He doesn't need you to interpret what God is telling him to do, but to support him in it and pray for him if he strays from it."

The same is true if the husband is unsaved. His spiritual life is in the Lord's hands. He does not need for his wife to "play" God for him, but to be a representative of God to him.

Most of us can think back to the time when we were unbelievers, or were so carnal that no one could tell the difference. We need to remember how offensive it was when anyone tried to approach us about the Lord.

I recall a time when I was so deeply involved in sin that I wasn't giving so much as a thought to the things of God. I was worried because my daughters were going to vacation Bible school at a church where they pushed Bible reading, talked too much about Jesus, and had altar calls. I didn't want my children to become fanatics.

During that same period of time, I received a letter from my cousin, telling me about the peace God had given her when her brother died. She quoted Scripture and rejoiced about their being together in eternity. I was so appalled that I actually made fun of the letter. I was so sinful that I was totally unresponsive to spiritual things; I was even repulsed by them.

The unbelieving husband probably feels that way. So if his wife, who claims to love him and want what is best for him, tries to force spiritual issues, he will balk, at both her and God. She needs to maintain a low profile about the Lord and spiritual matters. She needs to understand when he is disinterested or even belligerant about church, Bible studies, and her relationship with the Lord. It is reasonable for him to be unreasonable about her lifestyle.

EXPECT PROBLEMS AS A PART OF LIFE

Remember, an unequally yoked wife may have a tendency to idealize Christian marriages and possibly blame many normal problems on the fact that her husband is unsaved. This is a false assumption and can cause irreparable damage to the relationship.

The truth is that many of the problems the unequally yoked wife faces in her marriage are common to all marriages and are not solely due to the fact that her husband is not a Christian. People are people. We all have strengths and weaknesses, faults and virtues. Some Christian husbands have tempers and are at times unreasonable and unappreciative and disobedient to the Lord. Christian couples argue, disagree, and act selfishly.

In a setting as intimate as marriage, where every facet of an individual's personality and character are shared, and in some ways are infringed upon by another, there will be conflict and, sometimes, disorder. The major difference between the Christian couple who has problems and an unequally yoked situation is that both believers are indwelt by the Holy Spirit. He is an inner controlling factor in the overall relationship.

Millie shared that she assumed that every problem she and Tom had in their marriage was due to the fact that he was not a Christian. No matter what difficulties they faced, she dismissed any personal responsibility because she was saved and he was not.

So when he blew up at her for spending too much money, and it happened to be a time when she had given a generous amount to a missionary fund, she wrote it off as his not wanting her to donate to the church.

As time passed, Tom repeatedly told her she had to cut back on expenditures. He finally informed her that he was going to give her a household and personal allowance instead of leaving the checkbook with her, so he could control what she spent.

She was furious! She called him selfish. She was raving because he threw away money on golf fees and beer. She was convinced he was persecuting her for being a Christian. When we talked, I suggested that she list, in detail, the purchases she had made in the past three months. She discovered that she was spending almost one-third of their net income on whatever she wished, without even consulting her husband.

"I know now that I purposely blamed Tom's unbelief so I would not have to face the fact that I am a spendthrift. I was causing our financial problems and didn't want to accept the responsibility for it." The unequally yoked wife has to be careful not to use "he's not a Christian" as a cop-out for her failings.

LOOK FOR POSITIVES

Although every unbeliever is an unregenerated sinner, that does not mean that he is a reprobate. George and I have often talked about how the only noticeable change in his life, after he accepted the Lord, was his inclination toward spiritual things. Even before he became a Christian, George was a good man. He was gentle, kind, honest, dependable, and had a sense of humor. That's why I married him.

A Christian wife should look for positive character and personality assets in her unsaved husband. What qualities made her want to marry him in the first place? In what ways is he maturing and growing? What are some things he does that please her and make her happy?

When I teach, I sometimes ask the class to list five things they dislike about their husbands. When the lists are completed, I ask them what they think would happen in their marriages if they spent an hour a day dwelling on each negative they have recorded. After the laughter subsides, we conclude that if we spent time thinking about our husband's faults we could make ourselves miserable within a period of a few hours.

Next, I suggest that they look at every fault on the list, pray about it, and submit it to God. Then they should tear up the list and, through an act of their will, erase those things from their minds.

Finally, we make a list of positives about our husbands. Each woman plans to concentrate on and compliment her husband about at least one of those facets during the next week. When the women return to class, the ones who have worked toward this goal tell glowing stories about the warm, loving responses they are getting from their mates.

An unequally yoked wife must not get lost in negatives, especially the fact that her husband is not saved. She should look for, hope for, and expect the best.

BE GENUINE

The world is inundated with phonies, hypocrites: men and women who say one thing and do another. Webster defines a hypocrite as someone who pretends to be better than he really is, or who pretends to be pious or virtuous without really being so.

In the twenty-third chapter of Matthew, the Lord delivers a scathing rebuke against religious hypocrites. He calls them fools, blind guides, whitewashed tombs, vipers, and serpents. Repeatedly, He addresses them as hypocrites. The Greek word for hypocrite means "actor." He indicts them for being phonies; for playacting at being godly.

The world responds much the way Christ did to religious hypocrisy. So will an unbelieving husband. Therefore, the unequally yoked wife must act out her Christianity in sincerity and with conviction. What she does, or does not do, will affect her husband's opinion of what he thinks a Christian should be.

For instance, is the wife judgmental? Even unbelievers know

Christians are not supposed to judge others. Does she use earthy language? Is she unreasonably impatient with the children? And what about her relationships with the neighbors and her husband's friends? Is she super-critical, aloof, and pious, or does she minister to them with a servant's heart?

The apostle John observed that "the one who says he abides in Him ought himself to walk in the same manner as He walked" (1 John 2:6). An unbelieving husband has a right to expect his Christian wife to emulate Christ and to fault her if she does not.

BE LOYAL

When Bathsheba gave her son, Solomon, advice on how to choose a wife, she placed faithfulness at the top of the list of admirable, wifely attributes. She counseled her son that an excellent wife (who, incidentally, is hard to find) is so dependable that "the heart of her husband [can trust] her, and he will have no lack of gain. She does him good and not evil all the days of her life" (Prov. 31:11-12).

We have already seen that this kind of faithfulness goes beyond mere physical fidelity, to the depths of the soul. A husband should be able to trust his wife with his *heart:* his emotions, his will, his awareness, his intellect—with his total being. And, a godly wife will always and forever look out for her husband's best interests.

An unequally yoked wife can do her husband immeasurable harm by advertising the fact of his unbelief. I am not saying she should keep it a secret, but she must keep it in perspective. Marriage is a covenant between two people and the Lord, even if one or both of them do not have a personal relationship with Him. In our society, when someone makes a legal contract, he is expected to carry out its terms to the best of his ability.

The same is true in a marriage. God's stipulations are unconditional. A wife is to be loyal to her husband, unless there are extreme extenuating circumstances. Those must be dealt with as exceptions, not as the rule.

What does wifely loyalty involve? Basically, it means she sees, hears, and speaks no evil about the man to whom she is married. She puts *his* best foot forward in the way she talks about him and the way her attitudes portray their relationship. The things a wife implies or tells others about her mate reflects on her. "Be to his virtues very kind; be to his faults a little blind," is good advice.

PUT GOD FIRST

There is no doubt that the unequally yoked wife is in a precarious position. There will be times when she has to choose between her husband and her God. She must adhere to the principle that *in all things Christians are commanded to put God first.*

When Peter and the apostles were hauled before the council and threatened with imprisonment, they testified, "We must obey God rather than men" (Acts 5:29). The principle *all* believers are required to follow is that we are to put God and His law before any man or man-made law.

Although the concept is simple, acting it out is not. The unequally yoked wife cannot assume arbitrarily, in all situations, to know what God wants. So she has to evaluate each decision in the light of that standard. The best way to approach gray areas is to look at Christ's example. What did He do in similar predicaments? Is there a specific command in Scripture regarding the circumstances? Will what she is being asked to do strengthen or weaken her witness? And, most of all, will it please her husband without detracting from Christianity? Remember, there is a monumental difference between self-righteousness and the righteousness of God!

RELY ON THE CHARACTER OF GOD

Ultimately, everything any Christian does must be viewed in the light of the character of God. No theology will work if it is not intrinsically related to the One who established it. Too often we are trapped by our own lack of faith into looking at our circumstances instead of at our Lord, who is Master of all things.

It is important that an unequally yoked wife understand how

God's attributes relate to her protection and well-being. God is *sovereign,* so nothing can or will happen to her that He does not direct or permit. She is in His hands.

God is *immutable.* He never changes. If He was capable of delivering His saints in the past and saving them from their sin, He can still guide and protect an unequally yoked wife, no matter how intense or unhappy the situation.

God is *omnipresent.* He is always with her, even in the most heated or unpleasant times in the marriage. He will never leave her. He is *omnipotent,* so He can control even the most impossible of situations. He spoke and the world came into being. His power is complete, infinite, unlimited. He can act, speak, and invade enemy territory on her behalf and accomplish what He wishes, when He wants.

God is *perfect justice;* impartial and fair in all His dealings. He makes perfect decisions without bias. Therefore, anything He chooses to let happen to her will be fair and for her welfare.

God is *love.* Therefore, when she is rejected, hurt, and feeling unappreciated, she can turn to Him and He will compassionately respond to her needs. God is *merciful.* He does not give her what she deserves; He bestows lovingkindness, not condemnation. He also is *gracious,* so when her human resources break down, God is there to pour out His riches and blessing.

God is *faithful.* He is dependable and has set standards that never vary. He will keep every promise He has made. He will never let her down. He will undergird and support her even if everything else collapses. He is her God and He is there.

God is *wise* and *omniscient.* He never misuses His position. He has total insight and perfect discernment. He knows things she will never know, including the end from the beginning, so He is better qualified to manage her life than she is. And, God is *patient.* That is why He overlooks her mate doing things that she finds intolerable. That is why, when she wishes God would knock her husband to his knees and make him pray to be saved, He endures, waits, and is serenely diligent. He uses restraint when He is provoked, because He is longsuffering.

Because God is *eternal,* time does not matter to Him as it does to us. When we want something, we want it yesterday. But God is so great, so vast, so unfathomable that He is not limited in any aspect of His being. Time does not engulf Him. Our selfish demands do not sway Him. His motive always is love.

Every unequally yoked wife can rest in the fact that her destiny, and that of her husband and family, is in the hands of an infinite, magnificent God and that she is not at the mercy of her circumstances. She can control her situation by trusting the Lord and by doing what He has commanded. She can be happy, even if she is unequally yoked.

Workshop

1. Look up the Scripture verses under each heading and summarize the basic idea in your own words by completing the sentences.

   a. The unequally yoked wife can expect to be happy [blessed] if she:

      (1) *Psalm 128:1-2.* _____

      _____

      (2) *Psalm 146:5.* _____

      _____

      (3) *Proverbs 3:13.* _____

      _____

      (4) *Matthew 5:3.* _____

      _____

      (5) *1 Peter 3:14.* _____

      _____

   b. An unbeliever will be unreasonable about spiritual matters because:

      (1) *Romans 10:3.* _____

      _____

      (2) *Romans 8:7.* _____

      _____

c. Some practical ways an unequally yoked wife can act submissively are:

(1) *1 Corinthians 10:31-33.* _____

_____

(2) *Galatians 5:16.* _____

_____

(3) *Ephesians 4:1-3.* _____

_____

(4) *Ephesians 5:2.* _____

_____

d. According to these verses, some basic characteristics that deserve respect are:

(1) *Proverbs 31:30.* _____

_____

(2) *Ecclesiastes 5:2.* _____

_____

(3) *Matthew 20:26.* _____

_____

(4) *Philippians 2:3-4.* _____

_____

e. Some benefits derived from problems are:

(1) *Ecclesiastes 7:3.* _____

_____

(2) *Romans 5:3-4.* _____

_____

(3) *James 1:2-4.* _____

_____

(4) *1 Peter 1:7.* _____

_____

2. List five positives you appreciate about your husband.

a. _____

_____

b. _____

_____

c. _____

_____

d. _____

_____

e. _____

_____

3. You should praise your husband honestly for his good attributes because:

a. *Proverbs 15:4.* _____

_____

b. *Proverbs 16:24.* _____

_____

c. *Proverbs 15:23.* _____

_____

4. Read Proverbs 31:10-31 and list at least ten characteristics of a faithful, godly wife.

   a. _____

   b. _____

   c. _____

   d. _____

   e. _____

   f. _____

   g. _____

   h. _____

   i. _____

   j. _____

Don'ts for Marital Happiness

In recent years we've heard a lot about the power of positive thinking, but there is also such a thing as the power of negative thinking. Just as there are ways we should act and think, there are also things we shouldn't think or do. In the first psalm, David noted that we will be happy if we refrain from certain behavior: "How blessed is the man who does *not* walk in the counsel of the wicked, *nor* stand in the path of sinners, *nor* sit in the seat of scoffers!" (Ps. 1:1).

All but two of the Ten Commandments, which are mankind's basic code of moral and religious conduct, are "do nots." You shall *not* have other gods before God, make idols or worship them, take the name of the Lord in vain, murder, commit adultery, steal, bear false witness, or covet.

This is how the power of negative thinking works: There are things a godly wife must not do, things which, when she abstains from doing them will, through their absence, bring blessing. In this chapter we will review and expand on some of those things, which a Christian wife should not do if she wants the Lord to bless her marriage.

DON'T PUT UP COMMUNICATION BARRIERS

As we noted when we examined 1 Peter 3, the unequally yoked wife is not supposed to "talk" her husband to Christ or use the Bible as a weapon to try to get him to change his evil ways, but neither should she put up communication barriers in other areas. Marriage is a partnership where the intellect and emotions must be shared, as well as bodies and abodes. Marriage is a relationship in which two people are free to divulge their views, concerns, feelings, and expectations.

Also, some unequally yoked wives carry the command to win their husbands "without a word" (1 Peter 3:1) to extremes. While a wife is not supposed to verbally witness to her husband or hassle him with Scripture in order to make him repent, it is unrealistic to expect her never to mention to her husband the subjects of God, the church, her Christian friends, or religious activities. The Lord is part of her life and that certainly will reflect in what she says. She cannot pretend God doesn't exist.

There is a difference between quoting, "Be not drunk with wine" (Eph. 5:18 KJV) when her husband pours a glass of chablis at dinner and telling him something that happened at Bible study. Running around shouting "Praise the Lord" is different than sharing something she did at a church function. A wife should know her husband well enough to be able to tell what offends him and what does not.

Communication is an art; it has to be developed. Some of the best "how to" advice I ever got on the topic came from a sweet, Christian grandma who had been married to an unbeliever for forty-three years. She taught me what she called three ear openers: look, love, and listen.

She said that when you want to tell someone something, whether it's good news or bad, first you should *look* at him and see if he is ready to hear what you have to say. "Read" his eyes and facial expression; sense his mood. Take into account what he is doing right at that moment.

Next, whatever you say, say it with *love.* Love doesn't shout or nag; it corrects without condemning, and counsels without demanding its own way. Finally, you have to be willing to *listen* ("With your mouth tight shut," according to my surrogate grandmother) to whatever a person says back to you, whether you want to hear it or not. And remember, you can hear with your heart as well as your ears.

Beyond that wise philosophy, an unequally yoked wife will be better equipped to communicate with her husband if she understands that *conflict* is a basic part of the communication process. You may be familiar with Mrs. Billy Graham's famous observation that, in a marriage, if two people always agree, one of them is unnecessary.

Solomon, in his wisdom, noted that, "Iron sharpens iron, so one man sharpens another" (Prov. 27:17). We get hung up on conflict because we've been conditioned to believe that it is bad, even sinful. It is not. It is a tool God uses to help us mature. It's our reactions to conflict—anger, defensiveness, judgmentalism —that are the problem. So, if a Christian can understand what conflict is and how to handle it, she will be better prepared to cope with it in her marriage.

H. Norman Wright explains it in this way. "What is conflict? For some the word conjures up scenes of battlegrounds and warfare. This is not always true. . . . When conflict comes, it should be faced with the understanding that disagreements do not mean an entire relationship is on the verge of breaking down."[1]

Each of us is an individual. Each was created unique and different. No two people are alike. Also, each of us has a God-given ability to think, reason, and form opinions. Since we are all different, a certain amount of conflict in any relationship is normal. It is a natural outcropping of our created differences. An unequally yoked wife should expect a certain amount because of her and her husband's divergent spiritual beliefs. Instead of approaching it with an "I'm right" and "He's wrong" attitude, she should see it as "I'm a believer and my husband is not."

---

[1]H. Norman Wright, *Communication, Key to Your Marriage* (Glendale: Regal Books)

In Ephesians 4:29, God has outlined four standards for godly communication. His pattern is, "Let no unwholesome word proceed from your mouth, but only such as is good for edification, according to the need of the moment, that it may give grace to those who hear."

That short verse contains some basic qualifications for proper speech. One, whatever is said *must be wholesome:* pure and clean. Two, *it must edify the hearer,* not destroy his dignity, degrade him, or tear down his spirits. This doesn't mean it is wrong to criticize, but the criticism must be constructive, truthful, and spoken in love.

Three, the words that are spoken *must be appropriate.* Sometimes things need to be said, but not *when* we say them. Four, whatever is said *must give grace,* blessing, and pleasure to all who hear, even if what is being said was not meant for their ears.

So godly communication is wholesome, edifying, appropriate, and gracious, and if an unequally yoked wife employs the techniques taught in Scripture, she should be able to convey her thoughts and feelings to her unbelieving husband in an understandable, unthreatening way. What she says will open doors instead of erecting barriers.

The only communication limitation the Lord imposes is in the one area where an unbeliever lacks understanding, that of spiritual truth. Since an unsaved husband is not spiritually appraised, his Christian wife's knowledge in that sphere is to be communicated by her actions rather than through her words. This bond of silence will keep her from becoming proud over the fact that she grasps concepts which her husband cannot. It keeps her from becoming arrogant about her spirituality.

DON'T FLAUNT YOUR SPIRITUALITY

One of the most potent statements the Spirit directed the apostle Paul to make is: "Knowledge makes arrogant, but love edifies" (1 Cor. 8:1). And we Christians certainly are prone to be proud of what we know and to impose our superior interpretations of God's Word on everyone around us. An unequally yoked wife must be doubly cautious not to think of herself as better than her husband just because she knows Scripture and he does not. She may be more spiritually adept but she needs to use what she knows to build him up, not to put him down.

"I had a terrible time with this," Jenny said with a laugh. "I believe the Bible gives us God's perspective about how we should live and any time Roger said something that disagreed with my interpretation of Scripture, I'd contradict him and tell him he was wrong. I measured everything he said and did by my supposedly superior standards.

"Finally," she continued, "one Saturday one of my friends came over for coffee and Rog sat and talked with us about the world situation. When he left she asked me what was the matter with me; what was making me treat Roger that way. I was shocked. I honestly didn't know what she meant. She told me I'd taken exception to everything he'd said. What it boiled down to was I thought his idea about what should be done in the Middle East was stupid because it didn't fit in with my views on endtimes prophecy."

Jenny said she spent the next few days listening to herself and was ashamed of what she heard. "Fortunately, Rog didn't know why I was on his case so he didn't blame the Lord for the way I was acting. When I realized what I was doing, that I had a bad pride problem, thinking I knew so much, I made sure it never happened again."

The unequally yoked wife has to remember that she and her husband are both sinners; the variation is that she is saved and he is not. But that doesn't make him any less of a person or less deserving of dignity and respect.

DON'T BE DOGMATIC

One way she can squelch feelings of spiritual superiority is by avoiding dogmatism. When someone is convinced she is right, it's easy to be arbitrary. So, it is easy for a Christian wife, who knows God's truth, to become dogmatic about her beliefs.

Not too long ago I heard a pastor say that he is convinced that the only doctrine in Scripture on which all true believers agree is that we have to believe on the Lord Jesus Christ to be saved. A step beyond that, he noted, some think you receive Him silently, by making a commitment in your heart; others by being baptized in water; and some may say conversion happens when a person speaks in tongues. Still others believe it takes place only when someone makes a public confession of faith, and every group can back up their views with Scripture. His point was that dogmatism can be deadly if carried beyond basic convictions.

Sue Ellen shared that she had been dangerously dogmatic about where she and her husband should go to church. She constantly prayed for Rick's conversion and was elated when, with no prodding, he told her he wanted to go to church with her one Sunday. The sermon that day happened to be about tithing, and Rick saw it as a "hype for money." He told his wife how he felt and suggested that perhaps they could go somewhere else the following week.

Instead of being thrilled that he wanted to go to church again, despite what had been an unsatisfactory experience for him, Sue Ellen tried to defend the pastor, explaining that he seldom preached about money. "I remember telling him, besides, what he said was right and I love that church and all my friends go there. I wanted him to go to *my* church, so he could learn their doctrine. I begged him to go there with me just one more time, but he wouldn't. Would you believe *I* got mad at *him* for being stubborn?" she said, laughing.

Sue Ellen said that as she started praying, the Holy Spirit convicted her about her attitude and what she had said. "Looking back, I couldn't believe I had been so dogmatic. Here I'd been waiting for years for a break like that. Then I didn't recognize that God was answering my prayers, and leading us to a church of His choosing, when He dropped it in my lap."

She said that she knows she should have been so grateful that she would have gone to church anywhere, if Rick was willing to go, too. "Somewhere in the back of my mind I'd always assumed that if he started going to church it would be where I was already a member. That was the way I wanted it, but God had other plans."

While such an assumption is understandably normal, it is not necessarily right. An unequally yoked wife must keep in mind that what matters spiritually is that her husband place his faith in Christ and acknowledge him as Savior, not that he go to her church or do it her way or interpret every doctrine as she does. She must be open-minded, rejecting prejudices and stereotypes, eliminating preconceived ideas that are based on habit and conjecture rather than fact.

If an unequally yoked wife is open-minded, rather than legalistic, she will be more approachable and less threatening to her husband. She doesn't have to compromise her beliefs but she should be willing to respect, allow for, and examine those which differ from hers, even if she knows they are incorrect.

DON'T SECOND-GUESS GOD

If an unequally yoked wife is open-minded, she will not nurture preconceived ideas about how or when the Lord will bring her unsaved husband into the fold. She should not try to second-guess God's plan or timing in her husband's salvational process. There is no way she can know when, how, or if he will come to Christ, so if she anticipates what God, or her husband, is going to do, she will be frustrated and disappointed.

Monica was certain if she could just get Jeff to listen to a certain tape, read a specific Christian book, or go to some church function, he would accept Christ. So she was always manipulating to make that happen. She'd leave books lying around, open to the page she wanted him to read. She'd loudly play the tapes she decided he needed to hear, hoping he would listen to what was being said. And, she was always asking him to go to some church dinner or program with her.

It didn't work. He never looked at any of the books. The only portions of the tapes he ever seemed to hear were the parts with which he disagreed. And although he sometimes went to church functions with Monica, it was like any other social outing to him.

Consequently, Monica was always disappointed. She'd get depressed because Jeff didn't respond the way she wanted him to. Each time she suffered a letdown, she blamed her husband and eventually ended up angry at him because he didn't do what she thought he should. That would be an easy trap to fall into.

In 1 Corinthians, chapter 7, after Paul has given the marriage guidelines and confirmed that if an unbelieving mate chooses to leave, the Christian is freed from the relationship, he makes this statement: "For how do you know, O wife, whether you will save your husband?" (1 Cor. 7:16). He is pointing out that there is no way a Christian wife can know if God plans to use her as the instrument of her husband's salvation. Chances are, if He allows the unbeliever to leave, He is not. But, she *cannot* know! How could she? How can anyone? If she assumes she does know, then she will do what Monica did and try to usurp the role of the Holy Spirit. Or, if the marriage has deteriorated to the place that the unbeliever wants to leave, she will try to hang on to a relationship that should be terminated. A wife doesn't have to stay with an unsaved husband so she can save him.

Marion shared her perspective. She was married to Frank for thirty-seven years. He never accepted Christ. "Knowing he would go to hell when he died bothered me a great deal. At first I tried to discuss God's Word with him many times, until he simply said he didn't believe as I did and never would. Since I wasn't able to alter his opinion, I did what I was sure God wanted me to do. I tried to be patient and live a good Christian example. I loved and cared and prayed he would change and believe Jesus was the way, the truth, and the light.

"That never happened," she continued. "For thirty-seven years I longed and prayed that Frank might become a believer. I wanted it for him; I wanted it for myself; I wanted it for us. But after he told me he would never believe as I do, I just knew I had to leave him in God's hands. I did all I could. The Lord did all He could, but Frank never accepted Christ."

Marion says she is glad that she didn't live her life anticipating her husband's conversion. "I just tried to have a congenial relationship with him in other areas and enjoy every day for what it was, so I have a lot of good memories. I concentrate on those and try not to think about the fact that Frank is in hell. But when I do, the Lord reminds me he's there as a result of his sin, not mine."

Marion has peace because she accepted God's will for her husband's role in their marriage, even though she didn't know what would happen concerning his salvation. She didn't try to force her spirituality on him or dictate what God should do. An unequally yoked wife must be careful not to make assumptions about what, when, how, or if the Lord will do something in her husband's life. She must never presume on God by thinking she can determine or control how or when her husband will become a Christian.

DON'T EXPECT MERCY WITHOUT JUSTICE

Finally, a Christian woman cannot expect God to honor her disobedience if she willfully married an unbeliever. She should expect to be disciplined and accept it as part of her growth. She must realize that the Lord isn't disciplining her to get back at her for marrying out of His will, but to lead her into future obedience.

She may not like what happens, but she should keep it in perspective: "All discipline for the moment seems not to be joyful, but sorrowful." It may not be pleasant, but it serves a purpose: "Yet to those who have been trained by it, afterwards it yields the peaceful fruit of righteousness" (Heb. 12:11). God's discipline is training in righteousness; it is how He teaches His children to become spiritual adults. And it doesn't last forever. There is an afterwards.

The key to enduring God's discipline is acceptance. "Do not reject the discipline of the LORD, or loathe His reproof" (Prov. 3:11). Rather than making excuses and balking at what the Lord is doing in her life, if an unequally yoked wife will openly receive what God has for her, she will better adapt to her marriage and her husband. She must believe He is doing it in love, "For whom the LORD loves He reproves, even as a father, the son in whom he delights" (Prov. 3:12).

Also, an unequally yoked wife must remember that God doesn't make her husband sin, or purposely make her life miserable because she disobeyed. Connie noted that, "Mostly, God's discipline has come packaged in my reaping what I sowed. I knew Kent drank before I married him. I knew he was extravagant. Now, I have to live with a party-boy who spends our money much too readily on the wrong things. That's not God's fault. But His discipline is that every time I balk or complain, He reminds me that's the price I'm paying for my self-indulgence.

"I am learning a lot from living with the consequences of my sin," she continued, "and so is Kent. The Lord uses His discipline to get our attention and point out problems, so we can work harder at building our marriage in a positive way." Connie has learned to accept and use God's discipline as a powerful, formative force in her life.

An unequally yoked wife will be more satisfied in her marriage and more accepting of her husband if she uses the power of negative thinking: if she *does not* build communication barriers, feel or act spiritually superior, be dogmatic, or try to second-guess the Lord's plans for her husband's life. She must learn to appreciate His loving discipline, live in the now, accept the relationship for what it is, and believe she can be happy when she refrains from doing things which will block God's blessing.

Workshop

1. Read Esther 5:1-8 and 7:1-4. In these passages the queen communicates a need to her husband. Write six words that describe her attitude when she approached him.

   a. _____

   b. _____

   c. _____

   d. _____

   e. _____

   f. _____

2. Look up and read each passage, then write a communication concept that is found in it.

   a. *Psalm 12:1-4.* _____

   _____

   b. *Psalm 19:14.* _____

   _____

   c. *Psalm 39:1.* _____

   _____

   d. *Psalm 59:12.* _____

   _____

e. *Psalm 63:11.* _____

_____

f. *Psalm 141:3.* _____

_____

g. *Proverbs 4:24.* _____

_____

h. *Proverbs 10:31-32.* _____

_____

3. What's your communication quotient? Rate yourself on a scale of 1-10, 10 being best. Look up the Scripture verse if one is listed.

   a. I pray for wisdom and discernment in our relationship. (James 1:5) _____
   b. I listen *to* my husband, not *at* him. _____
   c. I know about and understand his interests and am generally knowledgeable about them even though I am not involved myself. _____
   d. I wait for explanations rather than jumping to conclusions. (Prov. 29:20) _____
   e. I truthfully and fully share my thoughts and opinions with him. _____
   f. I respect and accept his silence when he doesn't speak. _____
   g. I am sensitive to my husband's needs and consider how he feels before I talk with him. _____
   h. I tell my husband when I disagree and why. _____
   i. I think before I answer. (Prov. 18:13; 15:28) _____
   j. I am as quick to compliment as I am to criticize. (Prov. 16:24) _____

4. How open-minded are you? Rate yourself on a scale of 1-10.

    a. I evaluate all new ideas that are presented to me.   _____

    b. I check facts to be sure they are correct.   _____

    c. I like to learn new things, even if it means changing my previous opinions.   _____

    d. I am fair in my judgments and decisions.   _____

Ministering to the Unequally Yoked

There is no denying that Christian women who are unequally yoked face some different kinds of problems in their marriages than those who are married to believers. There are many similarities in all marriages, but Christian husbands have been commanded by the Lord to "love [their] wives, just as Christ also loved the church and gave Himself up for her" (Eph. 5:25), "to love their own wives as their own bodies" (Eph. 5:28). They are accountable to the Lord and should "live with [their] wives in an understanding way, as with a weaker vessel, since she is a woman; and grant her honor as a fellowheir of the grace of life, so that [their] prayers may not be hindered" (1 Peter 3:7). And, God will discipline those who are not obedient in fulfilling their role.

Conversely, an unsaved husband is controlled by the world instead of the Holy Spirit. This cannot help but make a dramatic difference in the husband/wife relationship. God is not present in his life. No matter how moral and upright he is, he walks in spiritual darkness. This places a tremendous burden on his believing wife.

But that burden is not hers alone. It also belongs to the church. "We, who are many, are one body in Christ, and individually members one of another" (Rom. 12:5), so the problems these unequally yoked wives face become our corporate problems. Since we are to "bear one another's burdens" (Gal. 6:2) and "have the same care for one another [so] if one member suffers, all the members suffer with it; if one member is honored, all the members rejoice with it" (1 Cor. 12:25-26), it seems that all of us in the body must be more sensitive to these women (and men) who are in such a precarious position.

Oh, we're happy to pray for their husbands' salvation, and try to include them in social functions that aren't too religious in nature, but we don't minister to their gut-level needs. We should emphasize the commonness of our bonds in Christ and learn about their unique problems, literally bear the burden of their unsaved mates with them. In recent years the church has done this for singles, divorcees, and single parents. It is time we started ministering to the unequally yoked.

WHY START AN UNEQUALLY YOKED MINISTRY?

As we have seen, unequally yoked wives are spiritually isolated in some ways. They need to learn the principles taught in regular Bible classes, but they also need special instruction on how to apply them to their everyday lives. Sometimes they need to be with other women who have a "soul" identity with their problems and concerns. Yet very few churches do anything out of the ordinary to provide that kind of specialized fellowship and individualized instruction for the unequally yoked.

Paul told Titus that the older (in years, experience, and spiritual maturity) women are to teach the younger women, and first on the list of what that tutelage must include is that they be shown how "to love their husbands, to love their children" (Titus 2:4). On that basis, the women of the church have been given the responsibility to educate unequally yoked wives in those areas.

HOW TO START AN UNEQUALLY YOKED MINISTRY

Although there are many approaches to starting such a ministry, I'll share with you what a group of us initially devised, not because it's the only way to structure the beginnings of an un-equally yoked ministry, but because it worked.

Five of us women in the church got permission to see what we could develop. I was especially burdened because about half of the women in my regular, weekly Bible study were in that posi-tion. They were the ones who always had the most questions, the "what ifs," the deepest feelings of frustration. They obviously needed more counsel.

So the five of us formed a planning committee, which con-sisted of a single girl who was a seminary student at the time, two women who were unequally yoked, and two of us who were not. As we brainstormed and built on ideas we had gotten from another church that had a similar ministry, this is what we developed.

We did not want to segregate the unequally yoked women from regular Bible studies or church activities, so we decided to limit an unequally yoked class to once a month. Any special functions, like potluck dinners, theater parties, beach trips, or ball games, would be arranged intermittently, whenever they were feasible, to include husbands.

We wanted the ministry to be available to any Christian woman who was married to an unbeliever, including those who were employed. So we opted for a night meeting time, setting a stringent rule that class would start promptly at 7:00 PM and end at nine, so no husbands could balk about their wives being out until all hours attending church activities. We felt it was neces-sary to provide child care, so husbands wouldn't be saddled with baby sitting unless they wanted to.

Since no regular teacher was available, we decided to use sponsors for the ministry and have a different speaker each month. The topics would be based on the special needs of the group.

MONTHLY FORMAT

The following is a suggested format for such a class. The sponsors are responsible for selecting topics, arranging for speakers, mailing notices, taking role, keeping a running roster of members, and setting up the book and tape lending libraries. They also conduct the meetings and, along with volunteers from the class, plan supplementary husband/wife social activities.

Monthly Format for Unequally Yoked Class

ONE MONTH IN ADVANCE

Select the topic and arrange for a speaker/teacher. Have the guest speaker give you a small homework assignment to send home with the class, if possible. Speakers may include women Bible teachers, pastors, women who have been unequally yoked or still are, or people from other churches who have expertise in a specific area of interest to the unequally yoked. The topics are best chosen based on the needs of the group and by polling the women who attend.

TWO WEEKS IN ADVANCE

Confirm the date, time, and place with the speaker. Set up arrangements and place a notice about the class in the church bulletin. This should appear for two Sundays preceding class.

ONE WEEK IN ADVANCE

Mail class members a notice about the class. *Be sure* NEVER *to include the term unequally yoked in anything mailed to the homes.* This is extremely offensive to unsaved husbands.

WEEK OF THE MEETING

Assemble supplies, such as name tags, sign-up sheets, a statement of purpose handout (telling what the class is all about), suggested book and tape lists, and the resource lending library.

NIGHT OF THE MEETING

The sponsors should arrive at least fifteen minutes before starting time. They should set out material and be there to greet the speaker and class members. The members should sign in and put on name tags. Guests should be welcomed. Classmates can check out books or tapes before or after the meeting. Prayer request sheets and any additional material should be given out as the women arrive.

MEETING FORMAT

1. Begin promptly at 7:00 PM.

2. The sponsor should give a welcome and go over the statement of purpose, telling what the class is and why it exists.

3. Introduce guests.

4. Have five to ten minutes of fellowship, when members greet each other, one on one.

5. Opening prayer, by sponsor or speaker.

6. Speaker (lesson), approximately thirty minutes.

7. Discussion. First, have the entire group ask questions of the teacher and interact as a class. Then break into smaller groups for more intimate discussion. This is when the women share their problems and learn practical application of what is being taught. It is their sharing time.

8. Group prayer. The women in the smaller groups will give prayer requests to each other and covenant to pray for one another. Important requests can be stated for the whole class. Some women may ask others to be prayer partners.

Try to finish on time so husbands are not upset by their wives staying out too late at a church function.

Purposes of an Unequally Yoked Ministry

An unequally yoked ministry has many purposes. We've already mentioned two: to provide a setting where women can share and interact with Christian sisters of like circumstances, and to minister to the special needs of unequally yoked wives. The ministry also provides a base for initial biblical instruction.

Women who are married to unbelievers can be taught how to be First-Peter-Three wives, understand their role and spiritual responsibilities, and receive practical instruction in the application of Scripture. Beyond that, counselors and classmates will be available to give advice about the problems they face. The ministry will be a source of prayer support.

Another important phase is outreach. The unequally yoked class can be a basis for social functions and provide fellowship opportunities which include the unsaved husbands. As long as they are not held at the church and exclude formal prayer time or Bible lessons, most husbands are more than happy to come. Frequently, this association with believers leads to involvement with the Lord.

"It's such a great idea," Lucy said, beaming. "Chuck and I can go out with *my* Christian friends and their husbands and I don't have to worry about anyone trying to pin him in a corner about God. I don't have to explain or make apologies if he smokes, says a swear word, or drinks a beer at the ball game. I just know that being around Christians, even if it's just for fun, has a positive effect."

The three specific purposes we established for our group were: 1) to see that the needs of the unequally yoked woman are met, 2) to direct her attention toward Jesus Christ and His plan for her life, and away from her problems and marriage situation, 3) to provide an environment where she can express herself, without embarrassment, with women of like circumstances.

MIRACLES HAPPEN!

As these needs are met and unequally yoked wives deepen their commitment to Christ and share, grow, and learn together, miracles happen! True miracles! The miracle of rebirth. As wives develop godly attitudes and relax in their marriages, as they are taught how to love their unsaved husbands, the Holy Spirit woos and wins them to the Lord.

Last spring the sponsors of the unequally yoked class sent out this announcement:

Dear Classmates:

It is with much praise and thanksgiving that I share with you that at our next meeting, Tuesday, March 20, at 7:00 PM, we will be having a GRADUATION CELEBRATION. We are losing two of our members. When one of our body rejoices, we all rejoice. Please come and hear the special testimonies of two of our friends whose husbands recently have come to know the Lord. You won't want to miss it. Our cup runneth over!

What other commendation does an unequally yoked ministry need?

What about you? What about your church? If you are unequally yoked, you need to be ministered to in the ways discussed in this chapter. You need to share with your sisters in Christ, and counsel and help them. Perhaps this isn't being done because no one knows the depth of your burden or what your special problems are. Why not tell someone? Ask for help. An unequally yoked ministry could be the answer to many of your difficulties. It might mean the difference between heaven and hell for some unsaved husbands. Why not give it a try? You have nothing to lose and eternal fruit to gain.

Workshop

Answer each question in your own words, basing your answer on what the verse says and on what you have read in this book.

1. *1 Peter 3:1-2.* How can a Christian wife witness to her unbelieving husband?

   _____

   _____

   _____

2. *Colossians 3:18.* How can an unequally yoked wife respect and submit to her husband when he is worldly?

   _____

   _____

   _____

3. *1 Thessalonians 5:17; Ephesians 5:18.* How can she develop a gentle and quiet spirit?

   _____

   _____

   _____

4. *2 Corinthians 2:14.* How can a Christian mother explain to her children why their father uses bad words, gets drunk, doesn't pray, or doesn't go to church, without undermining his position?

_____

_____

_____

_____

5. *1 Peter 3:15.* How can an unequally yoked wife overcome her husband's negative example to their children?

_____

_____

6. *Ephesians 4:15.* How can a Christian woman justify going to worldly social activities with her husband and mingling with unbelievers?

_____

_____